ANNA HAZARE:
Reformer, Socialist and Anti-Corruption Leader

ANNA HAZARE:
Reformer, Socialist and Anti-Corruption Leader

J C DUA

2011
Kaveri Books
New Delhi - 110 002

First Published in 2011
ISBN : 978-81-7479-121-4

First Published in 2011 by
Kaveri Books
4832/24, Ansari Road, Darya Ganj
New Delhi-110002 (India)
Tel: 011-23288140, 23245799
Telefax: 011-2382 8140
E-mail : kaveribooks@vsnl.com
E-mail : kaveribooks@gmail.com
web : www.kaveribooks.com

Typesetin Book Antiqua Font at
Delta Book World, New Delhi - 110 002

Printed at
G.S. Offset Printers, New Delhi

PRINTED IN INDIA

Preface

Anna Hazare is the face of India's fight against corruption. He has taken that fight to the corridors of power and challenged the government at the highest level. People, the common man and well-known personalities alike, are supporting him in the hundreds swelling to the thousands.

The villagers especially of native village revere him. Thakaram Raut, a school teacher in Ralegaon Siddhi says, "Thanks to Anna's agitations, we got a school, we got electricity, we got development schemes for farmers." Anna Hazare's fight against corruption began here. He fought first against corruption that was blocking growth in rural India. His organization - the Bhrashtachar Virodhi Jan Ando/ an (people's movement against Corruption). His tool of protest - hunger strikes. And his prime target - politicians.

His weapon is potent. In 1995-96,he forced the Sena-BJP government in Maharashtra to drop two corrupt Cabinet Ministers. In 2003, he forced the Congress-Nationalist Congress Party (NCP) state government to set up an investigation against four ministers. Maharashtra stalwarts like Sharad Pawar and Bal Thackeray have often called his style of agitation nothing short of "blackmail".

He is now fighting for the implementation *of* the Ian Lokpal Bill, an anti-corruption bill drafted by leading members *of* civil society that envisages speedy action in corruption cases against everyone, including ministers and senior bureaucrats.

More than 30 years after Anna Hazare started his crusade, as the 72-year old observes a hunger strike in Delhi against large-scale corruption at the national level, nothing really has changed except the scale of his battle.

However, it can safely be said that mature democracies have all gone through the stages we have, but in time that spans hundreds of years. Criminalized politics, mass prostitution and ill treatment of women, the poor and under-classes were all features of democracies whose societies are the envy of the world today. An anti-corruption movement requires far greater depth than the one that went into the Anna Hazare fast. It is not simply Lok Pal Act, but political, social and intellectual change must join hands together to move forward.

Dr. J. C. Dua

Contents

Introduction

The dream of India as a strong Nation will not be realized without self-reliant, self-sufficient villages, this can be achieved only through social commitment and involvement of the common man.

- Anna Hazare

In India, corruption has been a slow burning. However, in 2010, it flared up with the revelation of a spate of scams and scandals across the country. Today, Anna Hazare is the face of India's fight against corruption. He has taken that fight to the corridors of power and challenged the government at the highest level. People, the common man and well-known personalities alike, are supporting him in the hundreds swelling to the thousands.

Kisan Baburao Hazare popularly known as Anna Hazare, is an Indian social activist who is especially recognised for his contribution to the development of Ralegan Siddhi, a village in Pamer taluka of Ahmednagar district, Maharashtra, India and his efforts for establishing it as a model village, for which he was awarded in 1992 the Padma Bhushan - the third-highest civilian award- by the Government of India.

The villagers revere him. Thakaram Raut, a school teacher in Ralegaon Siddhi says, "'Thanks to Anna's agitations, we got a school, we got electricity, we got development schemes for farmers." Anna Hazare's fight against corruption began here. He fought first against corruption that was blocking growth in rural India. His organization is- the *Bhrashtachar Virodhi Jan Andolan* (people's movement against Corruption); his tool of protest - hunger strikes; and his prime target - Politicians.

On 05 April 2011 Hazare started a 'fast unto death' to exert pressure on the Government of India to enact a strong anti-corruption act as envisaged in the Jan Lokpal Bill, a law to establish a Lokpal (ombudsman) with the power to deal with corruption in public offices. The fast led to nationwide protests in support of Hazare. The fast ended on 09 April 2011, the day after all of Hazare's demands were agreed by the Government of India. The government issued a gazette notification on the formation of a joint committee (of government and civil society representatives) to draft an effective Lokpal Bill.

Anna Hazare was born on 15 January 1940 in Bhingar, a small village near the city of Ahmednagar, in Bombay Province (present-day Maharashtra). Hazare's father, Baburao Hazare, worked as an unskilled labourer in Ayurveda Ashram Pharmacy. Hazare's childless aunt offered to look after him and his education, and took Anna to Bombay (now known as Mumbai). Hazare studied up to the 7th standard in Bombay and then sought employment, due to the economic situation in his household. He started selling flowers at Dadar to support his family. He soon started his own shop and brought two of his brothers to Bombay. Gradually Hazare's income increased to around Rs. 800 per month, a decent income in those times.

Anna Hazare started his career in the Indian Army as a driver in 1963. He spent his spare time reading the works of Vivekananda, Gandhi, and Vinoba Bhave; they inspired him to become a social worker and activist. During the Indo-Pakistan War of 1965 he was the only survivor in a exchange of border fire while driving a truck in Khem Karan sector. During the mid-1970s he survived a road accident while driving.

After voluntary retirement from the army, Hazare went to Ralegan Siddhi village in 1975. Initially he organised the youth of the village into an organisation named the *Tarun Mandai.* He helped to form the *Pani Puravatha Mandals* to ensure proper distribution of water.

Hazare and the youth group next decided to take up the issue of alcoholism. At a meeting conducted in the temple, the villagers resolved to close down liquor dens and ban alcohol in the village. Since these resolutions were made in the temple, they became in a sense religious commitments. Over thirty liquor brewing units were closed by their owners voluntarily. Those who did not succumb to social pressure were forced to close down their businesses when the youth group smashed up their liquor dens. Hazare said, "Doesn't a mother administer bitter medicines to a sick child when she knows that the medicine can cure her child. The child may not like the medicine, but the mother does it because she cares for the child. The alcoholics were punished so that their families would not be destroyed."

His weapon is potent. In 1995-96, he forced the Sena-BJP government in Maharashtra to drop two corrupt Cabinet Ministers. In 2003, he forced the Congress-Nationalist Congress Party (NCP) state government to set up an investigation against four ministers. Maharashtra stalwarts like Sharad Pawar and Bal Thackeray have often called his style of agitation nothing short of "blackmail".

Hazare appealed to the Government of Maharashtra to bring in a law whereby prohibition would come into force in a village if 25% of the women in the village demanded it. In July 2009 the state government issued a government resolution amending the Bombay Prohibition Act, 1949. As per the amendments, if at least 25% of women voters demand liquor prohibition through a written application to the state excise department, voting should be conducted through a secret ballot. If 50% of the voters vote against the sale of liquor, prohibition should be imposed in the village and the sale of liquor should be stopped. Similar action can be taken at the ward level in municipal areas. Another circular was issued making it mandatory to get the sanction of the Gram Sabha for issuing new permits for the sale of liquor. In some instances, when women agitated against the sale of liquor, cases were filed against them. Hazare took up the issue again. In August 2009 the government issued another circular that sought withdrawal of cases against women who sought prohibition of liquor in their villages. It was also decided to ban the sale of tobacco and cigarettes in the village.

Ralegan is located in the foothills, so Hazare persuaded villagers to construct a watershed embankment to stop water and allow it to percolate and increase the ground water level and improve irrigation in the area. Residents of the village used *shramdan* to build canals, small-scale check-dams, and percolation tanks in the nearby hills for watershed development. These efforts solved the problem of water scarcity of water in the village and made irrigation possible.

In order to conserve soil and water by checking runoff, contour trenches and gully plugs were constructed along the hill slopes. Cultivation of water-intensive crops like sugar cane was banned. Crops such as pulses, oilseeds, and certain cash crops with low water requirements were grown. The farmers started growing high-yield varieties of crop and the cropping pattern of the village was changed. Hazare has helped farmers of more than 70 villages in drought-prone regions in the state of Maharashtra since 1975. The Government of India plans to start a training centre in Ralegan Siddhi to understand and implement Hazare's watershed development model in other villages in the country.

As a secondary occupation, milk production was promoted in Ralegan Siddhi. Purchase of new cattle and improvement of the existing breed with the help of artificial insemination and timely guidance and assistance by a veterinarian resulted in an improvement in the cattle stock. The number of milk cattle has also been growing, which resulted in growth from 100 liters (before 1975) to around 2,500 liters per day. Some milk is given to *Balwadi* children and neighbouring villages under the child nutrition program sponsored by the Zilla Parishad.

Hazare, along with the youth of Ralegan Siddhi, worked to increase literacy rates and education levels. In 1976 they started a pre-school and a high school in 1979. The villagers formed a charitable trust, the Sant Yadavbaba Shikshan Prasarak Mandal, which was registered in 1979. The trust obtained a government grant of Rs. 4 lakhs for the school building using the National Rural Education Programme. This money funded a new school building that was built over the next two months using volunteer labour. A new hostel was constructed to house 200 students from poorer sections of society. After the opening of the school, a girl from Ralegan Siddhi became the first female in the village to complete her Secondary School Certificate in 1982.

The Gandhian philosophy on rural development considers the Gram Sabha as an important democratic institution for collective decision making in the villages of India. Hazare campaigned between

1998 and 2006 for amending the Gram Sabha Act, so that the villagers have a say in the development works in their village. As per the amendments, it is mandatory to seek the sanction of the Gram Sabha for expenditures on development works in the village. Hazare was not satisfied as the amended Act did not include the right to recall a *Sarpanch*. He insisted that this should be included and the state government relented. In Ralegan Siddhi, in addition to the panchayat, there are several registered Societies that take care of various projects and activities of the village. In 1991, Hazare launched the *Bhrashtachar Virodhi Jan Aandolan* (BVJA), a popular movement to fight against corruption in Ralegaon Siddhi. In the same year he protested against the collusion between 40 forest officials and timber merchants. This protest resulted in the transfer and suspension of these officials. In May 1997 Hazare protested against alleged malpractices in the purchase of power looms by the Vasantrao Naik Bhathya Vimukt Jamati Vikas Manch and the Mahatma Phule Magasvargiya Vikas Mandal. These institutions were directly under the charge of then Maharashtra Social Welfare minister Babanrao Gholap of the Shiv Sena, since their managing committees were dissolved after the Shiv Sena-Bharatiya Janata Party government came to power in the state in 1995.

Hazare also raised the issue of an alleged massive land purchase by Gholap's wife Shashikala in Nashik between April and September 1996. He forwarded the available documentary evidence to then Maharashtra Governor P.C. Alexander. On 4 November 1997 Gholap filed a defamation suit against Hazare for accusing him of corruption. He was arrested in April 1998 and was released on a personal bond of Rs 5,000.

On 09 September 1998 Hazare was imprisoned in the Yerawada Jail to serve a three month sentence mandated by the Mumbai Metropolitan Court. The sentencing came as a huge shock at that time to all social activists. Leaders of all political parties except the BJP and the Shiv Sena came in support of him. Later, due to public protests, the Government of Maharashtra ordered his release from the jail. After release, Hazare wrote a letter to then chief minister Manohar Joshi demanding Gholap's removal for his role in alleged malpractices in the Awami Merchant Bank. Gholap resigned from the cabinet on 27 April 1999.

In 2003 corruption charges were raised by Hazare against four NCP ministers of the Congress-NCP government. He started his 'fast unto death' on 9 August 2003. He ended his fast on 17 August 2003 after then chief minister Sushil Kumar Shinde formed a one-man commission headed by the retired justice P. B. Sawant to probe his charges. The P. B. Sawant Commission Report, submitted on 23 February 2005, indicated Sureshdada Jain, Nawab Malik, and Padmasinh Patil. The Report exonerated Vijaykumar Gavit. The Report also indicted Hazare for corruption for the use of Rs. 2.20 lakh of funds from the Hind Swaraj Trust, which he heads, for his birthday celebrations, in spite of a subsequent donation of Rs. 2.48 lakh by industrialist Abhay Firodia to the trust for that purpose. Suresh Jain and Nawab Malik resigned from the Cabinet in March 2005.

But Anna Hazare has soldiered on relentless. From one battle to another in his war against corruption. He fought from the front to have Right to Information (RTI) implemented. In the early 2000s Hazare led a movement in Maharashtra state which forced the state government to pass a stronger Maharashtra Right to Information Act. This Act was later considered as the base document for the Right to Information Act 2005 (RTI), enacted by the Union Government. It also ensured that the President of India assented to this new Act.

Law Professor Alasdair Scott Roberts said: The state of Maharashtra - home to one of the world's largest cities, Mumbai, adopted a Right to Information Act in 2003, prodded by the hunger strike of prominent activist, Anna Hazare. "All corruption can end only if there is freedom of information," said Hazare, who resumed his strike in February 2004 to push for better enforcement of the Act.

On 20 July 2006 the Union Cabinet amended the Right to Information Act 2005 to exclude the file noting by the government officials from its purview. Hazare began his 'fast unto death' on 9 August 2006 in Alandi against the proposed amendment. He ended his fast on 19 August 2006, after the government agreed to change its earlier decision.

He is now fighting for the implementation of the Jan Lokpal Bill, an anti-corruption bill drafted by leading members of civil society that envisages speedy action in corruption cases against everyone, including ministers and senior bureaucrats.

More than 30 years after Anna Hazare started his crusade, as the 72-year-old observes a hunger strike in Delhi against large-scale corruption at the national level, nothing really has changed except the scale of his battle. On 5 April 2011 Hazare initiated a movement for passing a stronger anti-corruption Lokpal Bill in the Indian Parliament. Along with members of the India against Corruption movement, former justice of the Supreme Court of India and Lokayukta of Karntaka N. Santosh Hegde and Prashant Bhushan, a senior lawyer in the Supreme Court, drafted an alternate bill called the Jan Lokpal Bill. This bill provides more stringent provisions and wider power to the Lokpal. Hazare began a fast unto death from 05 April 2011 at Jantar Mantar in Delhi to press for the demand to form a joint committee of the representatives of the Government and the civil society to draft a new bill with stronger penal actions and more independence to the Lokpal and Lokayuktas.

The movement attracted attention in the media, and thousands of supporters. Almost 150 people reportedly joined Hazare in his fast. He said that he would not allow any politician to sit with him in this movement.

Social activists, including Medha Patkar, Arvind Kejriwal, and former IPS officer Kiran Bedi lent their support to Hazare's hunger strike and anti-corruption campaign. In addition to spiritual leaders Sri Sri Ravi Shankar, Swami Ramdev, Swami Agnivesh and former Indian cricketer Kapil Dev, many celebrities showed their public support through Twitter. On 06 April 2011 Sharad Pawar resigned from the group of ministers formed for reviewing the draft Lokpal Bill 2010.

The movement gathered significant support from India's youth, visible through the local support and on social networking sites. There have also been protests in Bangalore, Mumbai, Chennai, Ahmedabad, Guwahati, Shillong, and Aizawl, among other cities of India.

On 08 April 2011 the Government of India accepted all demands of the movement. On 09 April 2011 it issued a notification in the Gazette of India on formation of a joint committee. It accepted the formula that there be a politician Chairman and an activist, non-politician Co-Chairman. According to the notification, Pranab Mukheljee will be the Chairman of the draft committee while Shanti Bhushan will be the Co- Chairman. "The Joint Drafting Committee shall consist of five nominee ministers of the Government of India and five nominees of the civil society. The five nominee Ministers of the Government of India are Pranab Mukheljee, Union Minister of Finance, P. Chidambaram, Union Minister of Home Affairs, M. Veerappa Moily, Union Minister of Law and Justice, Kapil Sibal, Union Minister of Human Resource and Development and Minister of Communication and Information Technology and Salman Khursheed, Union Minister of Water Resources and Minister of Minority Affairs. The five nominees of the civil society are Anna Hazare, N. Santosh Hegde, Shanti Bhushan Senior Advocate, Prashant Bhushan, Advocate and Arvind Kejriwal.

On the morning of 09 April 2011 Hazare ended his 98-hour hunger strike by first offering lemon juice to some of his supporters who were fasting with him. Hazare then broke his fast by consuming some lemon juice. He addressed the people and set a deadline of 15 August 2011 to pass the Lokpal Bill in the Indian Parliament.

Real fight begins now. We have a lot of struggle ahead of us in drafting the new legislation. We have shown the world in just five days that we are united for the cause of the nation. The youth power in this movement is a sign of hope.

Anna Hazare said that if the Bill does not pass he will call for a mass nation-wide agitation. He called his movement as "second struggle for independence" and he will continue the fight.

In 2011, Anna Hazare demanded for an amendment to the electoral law to incorporate the option of "None of the above" in the electronic voting machines during the Indian elections. The "None of the above (NOTA)" is a ballot option that allows an electorate to indicate disapproval of all of the candidates in an electoral system, in case of non-availability of any candidate of his choice, as his Right to Reject. Soon, the Chief Election Commissioner Shahabuddin Yaqoob Quraishi supported Hazare's demand for the electoral reforms.

1

Anna Hazare: A Great Saint

Introduction

Kisan Baburao Hazare born on 15 January 1940, popularly known as Anna Hazare, is an Indian social activist who is especially recognised for his contribution to the development of Ralegan Siddhi, a village in Parner taluka of Ahmednagar district, Maharashtra, India and his efforts for establishing it as a model village, for which he was awarded the Padma Bhushan the third-highest civilian award by the government of India in 1992.

On 5 April 2011 Hazare started a 'fast unto death' to exert pressure on the government of India to enact a strong anti-corruption act as envisaged in the Jan Lokpal Bill, a law to establish a Lokpal (ombudsman) with the power to deal with corruption in public offices. The fast led to nationwide protests in support of Hazare. The fast ended on 9 April 2011, the day after all of Hazare's demands were agreed by the government of India. The government issued a gazette notification on the formation of a joint committee (of government and civil society representatives) to draft an effective Lokpal Bill.

Early Life

Anna Hazare was born on 15 January 1940 in Bhingar, a small village near the city of Ahmednagar, in Bombay Province (present-day Maharashtra). Hazare's father, Baburao Hazare, worked as an unskilled labourer in Ayurveda Ashram Pharmacy. His grandfather was in the army, posted at Bhingar, when Anna was born. He died in 1945 but Hazare's father continued to stay at Bhingar. In 1952, Hazare's father resigned from his job and returned to his own village, Ralegan Siddhi. Hazare had six younger siblings and the family faced significant hardships. Hazare's childless aunt offered to look after him and his education, and took Anna to Bombay now known as Mumbai.

Hazare studied up to the 7th standard in Bombay and then sought employment, due to the economic situation in his household. He started selling flowers at Dadar to support his family. He soon started his own shop and brought two of his brothers to Bombay. Gradually Hazare's income increased to around Rs. 800 per month, a decent income in those times.

Career in the Indian Army

Anna Hazare started his career in the Indian Army as a driver in 1963. He spent his spare time reading the works of Vivekananda, Gandhi, and Vinoba Bhave; they inspired him to become a social worker and activist. During the Indo-Pakistani War of 1965 he was the only survivor in a exchange of border fire while driving a truck in Khem Karan sector. During the mid-1970s he survived a road accident while driving.

Transformation of Ralegan Siddhi

After voluntary retirement from the army, Hazare went to Ralegan Siddhi village in 1975. Initially he organised the youth of the village into an organisation named the *Tarun Mandal* (Youth Association). He helped to form the *Pani Puravatha Mandal*s (Water Supply Associations) to ensure proper distribution of water.

Uprooting Alcoholism

Hazare and the youth group next decided to take up the issue of alcoholism. At a meeting conducted in the temple, the villagers resolved to close down liquor dens and ban alcohol in the village. Since these resolutions were made in the temple, they became in a sense religious commitments. Over thirty liquor brewing units were closed by their owners voluntarily. Those who did not succumb to social pressure were forced to close down their businesses when the youth group smashed up their liquor dens. The owners could not complain as their businesses were illegal.

Some villagers continued to drink in Ralegan Siddhi, as they obtained their liquor from neighbouring villages. The villagers decided that those men would be given three warnings, after which they would be physically punished. Twelve men who were found in a drunken state after warnings were tied to a pole with help from the youth group and flogged. Hazare said, "Doesn't a mother administer bitter medicines to a sick child when she knows that the medicine can cure her child? The child may not like the medicine, but the mother does it only because she cares for the child. The alcoholics were punished so that their families would not be destroyed."

Hazare appealed to the government of Maharashtra to bring in a law whereby prohibition would come into force in a village if 25% of the women in the village demanded it. In July 2009 the state government issued a government resolution amending the Bombay Prohibition Act, 1949. As per the amendments, if at least 25% of women voters demand liquor prohibition through a written application to the state excise department, voting should be conducted through a secret ballot. If 50% of the voters vote against the sale of liquor, prohibition should be imposed in the village and the sale of liquor should be stopped. Similar action can be taken at the ward level in municipal areas. Another circular was issued making it mandatory to get the sanction of the Gram sabha (the local self government) for issuing new permits for the sale of liquor. In some instances, when women agitated against the sale of liquor, cases were filed against them. Hazare took up the issue again. In August 2009 the government issued another circular that sought withdrawal of cases against women who sought prohibition of liquor in their villages.

It was decided to ban the sale of tobacco, cigarettes, and beedies (a speciality cigarette) in the village. In order to implement this resolution, the youth group performed a unique "Holi" ceremony twenty two years ago. The festival of Holi is celebrated as a symbolic burning of evil. The youth group brought all the tobacco, cigarettes, and beedies from the shops in the village and burnt them in a 'Holi' fire. Tobacco, cigarettes, or beedies are no longer sold in any shops at Ralegan Siddhi.

The Watershed Development Programme

Ralegan is located in the foothills, so Hazare persuaded villagers to construct a watershed embankment to stop water and allow it to percolate and increase the ground water level and improve irrigation in the area. Residents of the village used *shramdan* (voluntary labour) to build canals, small-scale check-dams, and percolation tanks in the nearby hills for watershed development. These efforts solved the problem of water scarcity of water in the village and made irrigation possible. The first embankment that was built using volunteer efforts developed a leak and had to be reconstructed, this time with government funding.

In order to conserve soil and water by checking runoff, contour trenches and gully plugs were constructed along the hill slopes. Grass, shrubs and about 3 lakh (300,000) trees were planted along the hillside and the village. This process was supplemented by afforestation, nullah bunds, underground check dams, and cemented bandhras at strategic locations. Ralegan has also experimented with drip and bi-valve irrigation. Papaya, lemon, and chillies have been planted on a plot of 80 acres (32 ha) entirely irrigated by the drip irrigation system. Cultivation of water-intensive crops like sugar cane was banned. Crops such as pulses, oilseeds, and certain cash crops with low water requirements were grown. The farmers started growing high-yield varieties of crop and the cropping pattern of the village was changed. Hazare has helped farmers of more than 70 villages in drought-prone regions in the state of Maharashtra since 1975. The Government of India plans to start a training centre in

Ralegan Siddhi to understand and implement Hazare's watershed development model in other villages in the country.

Milk Production

As a secondary occupation, milk production was promoted in Ralegan Siddhi. Purchase of new cattle and improvement of the existing breed with the help of artificial insemination and timely guidance and assistance by a veterinarian resulted in an improvement in the cattle stock. Milk production has increased. Crossbred cows are replacing local ones which gave a lower milk yield. The number of milk cattle has also been growing, which resulted in growth from 100 litres (before 1975) to around 2,500 litres per day. The milk is sent to a co-operative dairy (Malganga Dairy) in Ahmednagar. Some milk is given to *Balwadi* (kindergarten) children and neighbouring villages under the child nutrition program sponsored by the Zilla Parishad.

From the surplus funds generated, the milk society bought a mini-truck and a thresher. The mini-truck is used to transport milk to Ahmednagar and to take vegetables and other produce directly to the market, thus eliminating intermediate agents. The thresher is rented out to farmers during the harvesting season.

Education

In 1932 Ralegan Siddhi got its first formal school, a single classroom primary school. In 1962 the villagers added more classrooms through community volunteer efforts. By 1971, out of an estimated population of 1,209, only 30.43% were literate (72 women and 290 men). Boys moved to the nearby towns of Shirur and Parner to pursue higher education, but due to socioeconomic conditions, girls could not do the same and were limited to primary education. Hazare, along with the youth of Ralegan Siddhi, worked to increase literacy rates and education levels. In 1976 they started a pre school and a high school in 1979. The villagers formed a charitable trust, the *Sant Yadavbaba Shikshan Prasarak Mandal*, which was registered in 1979.

The trust obtained a government grant of Rs. 4 lakhs (400,000) for the school building using the National Rural Education Programme. This money funded a new school building that was built over the next two months using volunteer labour. A new hostel was constructed to house 200 students from poorer sections of society. After the opening of the school, a girl from Ralegan Siddhi became the first female in the village to complete her Secondary School Certificate in 1982. Since then the school has been instrumental in bringing in many of changes to the village. Traditional farming practices are taught in this school in addition to the government curriculum.

Removal of Untouchability

The social barriers and discrimination that existed due to the caste system in India have been largely eliminated by Ralegan Siddhi villagers. People of all castes come together to celebrate social events. The Dalits have been integrated into the social and economic life of the village. The villagers have built houses for the Dalits, and helped to repay their loans to free them from their indebtedness.

Collective Marriages

Most rural poor get into a debt trap as they incur heavy expenses at the time of marriage of their son or daughter. It is an undesirable practice but has almost become a social obligation in India. Ralegan's people have started celebrating marriages collectively. Joint feasts are held, where the expenses are further reduced by the *Tarun Mandal* taking responsibility for cooking and serving the food. The vessels, the loudspeaker system, the mandap, and the decorations have also been bought by the *Tarun Mandal* members belonging to the oppressed castes. From 1976 to 1986, 424 marriages have been held under this system.

Gram Sabha

The Gandhian philosophy on rural development considers the Gram Sabha as an important democratic institution for collective decision making in the villages of India. Hazare campaigned between 1998 and 2006 for amending the Gram Sabha Act, so that the villagers have a say in the development works in their village. The state government initially refused, but eventually gave in due to public pressure. As per the amendments, it is mandatory to seek the sanction of the Gram Sabha (an assembly of all village adults, and not just the few elected representatives in the gram panchayat) for expenditures on development works in the village. In case of expenditure without the sanction of the Gram Sabha, 20% of Gram Sabha members can lodge a complaint to the chief executive officer of the zilla parishad (the district-level governing body) with their signatures. The chief executive officer is required to visit the village and conduct an inquiry within 30 days and submit a report to the divisional commissioner, who has the power to remove the sarpanch or deputy sarpanch and dismiss the gram sevak involved. Hazare was not satisfied as the amended Act did not include the right to recall a sarpanch. He insisted that this should be included and the state government relented.

In Ralegan Siddhi, Gram Sabha meetings are held periodically to discuss issues relating to the welfare of the village. Projects like watershed development activities are undertaken only after they are discussed in the Gram Sabha. All decisions like *Nashabandi* (bans on alcohol), *Kurhadbandi* (bans on tree felling), *Charai bandi* (bans on grazing), and *Shramdan* were taken in the Gram Sabha. Decisions are taken in a simple majority consensus. The decision of the Gram Sabha is accepted as final.

In addition to the panchayat, there are several registered societies that take care of various projects and activities of the village. Each society presents an annual report and statement of accounts in the Gram Sabha. The *Sant Yadavbaba Shikshan Prasarak Mandal* monitors the educational activities. The *Vividh Karyakari Society* gives assistance and provides guidance to farmers regarding fertilizers, seeds, organic farming, and financial assistance. The *Sri Sant Yadavbaba Doodh Utpadhak Sahakari Sanstha* gives guidance regarding the dairy business. Seven co-operative irrigation societies provide water to the farmers from cooperative wells. The *Mahila Sarvage Utkarsh Mandal* attends the welfare needs of women.

Anti-corruption Protests in Maharashtra

In 1991 Hazare launched the *Bhraṣhtachar Virodhi Jan Aandolan* (BVJA) (People's Movement against Corruption), a popular movement to fight against corruption in Ralegaon Siddhi. In the same year he protested against the collusion between 40 forest officials and timber merchants. This protest resulted in the transfer and suspension of these officials.

In May 1997 Hazare protested against alleged malpractices in the purchase of powerlooms by the *Vasantrao Naik Bhathya Vimukt Jamati Vikas Manch* and the *Mahatma Phule Magasvargiya Vikas Mandal.* These institutions were directly under the charge of then Maharashtra Social Welfare minister Babanrao Gholap of the Shiv Sena, since their managing committees were dissolved after the Shiv Sena-Bharatiya Janata Party government came to power in the state in 1995. Hazare also raised the issue of an alleged massive land purchase by Gholap's wife Shashikala in Nashik between April and September 1996. He forwarded the available documentary evidence to then Maharashtra Governor P. C. Alexander. On 4 November 1997 Gholap filed a defamation suit against Hazare for accusing him of corruption. He was arrested in April 1998 and was released on a personal bond of Rs 5,000. On 9 September 1998 Hazare was imprisoned in the Yerawada Jail to serve a three month sentence mandated by the Mumbai Metropolitan Court. The sentencing came as a huge shock at that time to all social activists. Leaders of all political parties except the BJP and the Shiv Sena came in support of him. Later, due to public protests, the Government of Maharashtra ordered his release from the jail. After release, Hazare wrote a letter to then chief minister Manohar Joshi demanding Gholap's removal for his role in alleged malpractices in the Awami Merchant Bank. Gholap resigned from the cabinet on 27 April 1999.

In 2003 corruption charges were raised by Hazare against four NCP ministers of the Congress-NCP government. He started his 'fast unto death' on 9 August 2003. He ended his fast on 17 August 2003 after then chief minister Sushil Kumar Shinde formed a one-man commission headed by the retired justice P. B. Sawant to probe his charges. The P. B. Sawant commission report, submitted on 23 February 2005, indicted Sureshdada Jain, Nawab Malik, and

Padmasinh Patil. The report exonerated Vijaykumar Gavit. The report also indicted Hazare for corruption for the use of Rs. 2.20 lakh of funds from the *Hind Swaraj Trust*, which he heads, for his birthday celebrations, in spite of a subsequent donation of Rs. 2.48 lakh by industrialist Abhay Firodia to the trust for that purpose. Suresh Jain and Nawab Malik resigned from the cabinet in March 2005.

Right to Information Movement

In the early 2000s Hazare led a movement in Maharashtra state which forced the state government to pass a stronger Maharashtra Right to Information Act. This Act was later considered as the base document for the Right to Information Act 2005 (RTI), enacted by the Union Government. It also ensured that the President of India assented to this new Act. Law professor Alasdair Scott Roberts said:

The state of Maharashtra home to one of the world's largest cities, Mumbai, adopted a Right to Information Act in 2003, prodded by the hunger strike of prominent activist, Anna Hazare. ("All corruption can end only if there is freedom of information," said Hazare, who resumed his strike in February 2004 to push for better enforcement of the Act).

On 20 July 2006 the Union Cabinet amended the Right to Information Act 2005 to exclude the file notings by the government officials from its purview. Hazare began his 'fast unto death' on 9 August 2006 in Alandi against the proposed amendment. He ended his fast on 19 August 2006, after the government agreed to change its earlier decision.

Lokpal Bill Movement

On 5 April 2011 Hazare initiated a movement for passing a stronger anti-corruption Lokpal (ombudsman) bill in the Indian Parliament. Along with members of the India Against Corruption movement, former justice of the Supreme Court of India and Lokayukta of Karnataka N. Santosh Hegde and Prashant Bhushan, a senior lawyer in the Supreme Court, drafted an alternate bill called the Jan Lokpal Bill (People's Ombudsman Bill) This bill provides more stringent provisions and wider power to the *Lokpal* (Ombudsman). Hazare began a fast unto death from 5 April 2011 at Jantar Mantar in Delhi to press for the demand to form a joint committee of the representatives of the Government and the civil society to draft a new bill with stronger penal actions and more independence to the *Lokpal* and *Lokayuktas* (Ombudsmen in the states), after his demand was rejected by the Prime Minister of India Manmohan Singh. He stated, "I will fast until Jan Lokpal Bill is passed".

The movement attracted attention in the media, and thousands of supporters. Almost 150 people reportedly joined Hazare in his fast. He said that he would not allow any politician to sit with him in this movement. Politicians like Uma Bharti and Om Prakash Chautala were shooed away by protesters when they came to visit the site where the protest was taking place. Social activists, including Medha Patkar, Arvind Kejriwal, former IPS officer Kiran Bedi, and Jayaprakash Narayan lent their support to Hazare's hunger strike and anti-corruption campaign. In addition to spiritual leaders Sri Sri Ravi Shankar, Swami Ramdev, Swami Agnivesh and former Indian cricketer Kapil Dev, many celebrities showed their public support through Twitter. On 6 April 2011 Sharad Pawar resigned from the *group of ministers* formed for reviewing the draft Lokpal bill 2010.

The movement gathered significant support from India's youth, visible through the local support and on social networking sites like Facebook and Twitter. There have also been protests in Bangalore, Mumbai, Chennai, Ahmedabad, Guwahati, Shillong, and Aizawl, among other cities of India.

On 8 April 2011 the Government of India accepted all demands of the movement. On 9 April 2011 it issued a notification in the Gazette of India on formation of a joint committee. It accepted the formula that there be a politician Chairman and an activist, non-politician Co-Chairman. According to the notification, Pranab Mukherjee will be the Chairman of the draft committee while Shanti Bhushan will be the co-chairman. "The Joint Drafting Committee shall consist of five nominee ministers of the Government of India and five nominees of the civil society. The five nominee Ministers of the Government of India are Pranab Mukherjee, Union Minister of

Finance, P. Chidambaram, Union Minister of Home Affairs, M. Veerappa Moily, Union Minister of Law and Justice, Kapil Sibal, Union Minister of Human Resource and Development and Minister of Communication and Information Technology and Salman Khursheed, Union Minister of Water Resources and Minister of Minority Affairs. The five nominees of the civil society are Anna Hazare, N. Santosh Hegde, Shanti Bhushan Senior Advocate, Prashant Bhushan, Advocate and Arvind Kejriwal.

On the morning of 9 April 2011 Hazare ended his 98-hour hunger strike by first offering lemon juice to some of his supporters who were fasting with him. Hazare then broke his fast by consuming some lemon juice. He addressed the people and set a deadline of 15 August 2011 to pass the Lokpal Bill in the Indian Parliament.

Real fight begins now. We have a lot of struggle ahead of us in drafting the new legislation, We have shown the world in just five days that we are united for the cause of the nation. The youth power in this movement is a sign of hope.

Anna Hazare said that if the bill does not pass he will call for a mass nation-wide agitation. He called his movement as "second struggle for independence" and he will continue the fight.

❑❑❑

2

Improvement in Ralegan Siddhi Village

Introduction

Many great persons have cherished the dream of a strong nation after and even prior to India's Independence. In the pre-Independence period Swami Vivekananda devoted his entire life to the cause of building a new India. All his efforts were towards strengthening the nation and its religion. However he never defined religion in the narrow terms of Hindu, Muslim, Sikh or Jain but "Humanism" was the true religion for him. According to him the religion started from one's next door neighbour and unless one shared the grief and happiness of one's neighbour any religion would have no meaning. If a religion does not accord primary importance to compassion viz. giving food to a starving person or wiping the tears of widows then that is not a true religion according to Swami Vivekananda.

India gained freedom and after Independence great persons like Gandhi and Vinoba Bhave dreamt of a strong self sufficient country. They repeatedly stressed that if you want to build a strong nation, India's villages will have to be transformed since India is a country spread over villages. Hence to build a new India we will have to undertake the task of changing India's villages. Swami Vivekananda, Gandhi and Vinoba realized that without developing its villages the dream of building a new India cannot be attained; that is why they devoted every moment and everything of their life towards building this new society. They knew that unless there are more and more persons with social commitment, villages cannot be developed. Therefore they concentrated on creating new human heings by developing social commitment among the people. True democracy cannot be brought about by making laws or by government action. For that you need to bring about change at the societal Ievel as well as in the minds of its people. "To see God in every living being and to serve humanity is true religion" has always been told to us by our saints and seers. They also taught us to maintain purity and morality in our thought and actions as well as to drive vices away.

With these ideals in view, the work of rural development in the village Ralegan Siddhi was started in 1975. For the development of all the villages in India there should be at least one such village where development has touched every aspect of life. If such a village is created, then the people, social workers and the youth in many more villages will get inspiration as well as direction to start on the development path. Today a large number of villagers are facing the question as to what, precisely, they should do if they want to develop their villages. Many young men and women are also asking this question that they want to do something in their life but what should they do? They are searching for a proper direction. Many people in our villages believe that village development means a good building of the Gram Panchayat, a double storied building for the village credit society, surfacing of village roads and piped water supply in the village. But all this is not real development. Ultimately, the human beings for whom we construct those buildings in the village should undergo change. Their thoughts and actions have to be brought onto the right track. Until a human being realizes that besides living for oneself, one has a duty towards one's neighbour, one's village, one's society, and one's country, no real development can take place of the village people, or of the village or the country.

An effort for such real development has been made collectively by the people of Ralegan Siddhi. Programmes like ban on consumption of alcohol, eradication of untouchability, tree-plantation, family-planning, water harvesting and water conservation, community gobar-gas plant, agricultural development, irrigation by sprinklers, drip bi-valve irrigation, solar lights, solar heaters, solar pumps, windmill, community marriages, co-operative well irrigation schemes, construction of a building worth Rs. 15-20 lakh by *Shramadaan*, Grain Bank, improved horticulture, and many other schemes have been successfully implemented in this village.

The Ralegan Message

Planned development in India during the last four decades has contributed to the widening of the gulf between rural and urban areas of our country. There has never been a serious effort to develop the potentialities of the rural areas. In fact, the cities have developed at the cost of villages which have remained socially and economically underdeveloped. The cities have experienced a transportation revolution and are rapidly moving into the computer age. The industrial development has also been oriented to satisfy the needs of the demands of the richer sections of the urban population. Incomes in the urban areas are growing at a much faster rate than those in rural areas. In fact, there has been a decline in the real incomes of the rural poor. The recurring droughts have degraded the lands of the poor who cannot afford the means for new agricultural technology i.e. improved seeds, fertilizers and irrigation. Nor have the avenues of secondary employment grown. This process has led to the marginalisation of the poor and has resulted in increased migration to cities. It has been observed that a large number of rural families cannot survive without being supported by at least one member of the family working in the cities.

Ralegan Siddhi was one of the worst victims of this process when, in 1975 Anna Hazare a local resident started working in his own village. This village, Ralegan, eventually developed into a model village of Maharashtra. Ralegan has shown that when the people decide to take up their own development they can produce outstanding results with a little bit of support from the development bureaucracy. This village of about two thousand population in

Parner *taluka* of Ahmednagar district in Maharashtra has attracted wide attention, including that of the Planning Commission and of the Central Government. A ministerial delegation from China was taken to Ralegan to show them a model Indian village. A visit to Ralegan has become an essential component of the training programmes of MSW students, agricultural universities, trainee Block Development Officers, bank officers and IAS officers, not only of Maharashtra but also of other states. Though publicity or public attention is no measure of a project's importance, there are some unusual features which have given Ralegan a special place.

Anna Hazare did not have any background of specialized education or expertise in development issues. His selfless leadership and moral appeal mobilized the village youth. Other people in the village also came around in due course of time. The most remarkable aspect of Ralegan's economic development is that there have been no significant financial or managerial inputs from any industrial house or Indian Charitable institutions or foreign funding agencies. The entire development effort has been financed predominantly through well-known Government schemes of loans and assistance that are available to any other village. The mobilization of local people and their voluntary contribution of physical lahour (*Shramadaan*) as well as local ingenuity in adopting and implementing development schemes has been exemplary.

Reconstructing the moral fabric of the village and bringing them together was considered necessary before undertaking any development effort. Emotional unity was largely achieved by renovation of the village temple. The youth were mobilized by a campaign against alcoholism. The guiding principle of economic development adopted by the Ralegan people has been that of "growth with equity". Special attention was paid to eradication of social discrimination and to bring about greater economic equality by implementing special economic programmes for lower income groups.

Normally, economic development leads to widening of economic and social disparities. However in Ralegan, disparities within the village society have decreased rather than getting widened. Social development towards an egalitarian society has preceded as well as accompanied economic development in Ralegan.

The village people gave priority to integration of *Harijans* and other lower castesi nto the village community. This created a unified force and an unprecedented drive for undertaking development programmes. People from all sections in the village saw a stake in the development programmes because they knew that the fruits were distributed equitably and that everyone stood to gain without any discrimination.

Shramadaan is an essential component (worth Rs. 30/- for a government grant of Rs. 100/-) in the implementation of every program in the village. Whether it is digging a well, construction of check dams, planting of trees or building a hostel for the outstation students, one adult from every household contributed his/her free labour to the project. As a result the government grants for these schemes were utilized with 130 per cent results whereas thirty to sixty per cent leakage (misappropriation of funds/materials for personal benefit) is a common phenomenon elsewhere in India. The village has accepted a code of distribution of surplus generated by these development schemes. Fifty per cent of the returns goes to the beneficiaries, 25 per cent is utilized for repayment of loans and the balance 25 per cent goes towards raising reserve capital for taking up community benefit programmes in future.

Ralegan has not experimented in developing any new technologies. It has only implemented the well established ones. Even in the field of public health, safe drinking water supply, soak pits, gobar gas plants, smokeless *chulhas*, public latrines, public urinals, good exercise and nutritious food to all Balwadi and school going children have become part of Ralegan's life without any fanfare. As a result, the health status of the village including that of children and women has improved remarkably without any massive campaigns, curative camps or health care staff running around doing house to house check-ups.

Anna Hazare feels that individual morality and moral reconstruction of the village community are essential for laying the foundation of any worthwhile socio-economic development. He derives morality from religion, but without orthodoxy and superstition. Regular prayers, chanting of hymns and bhajans, reading of scriptures and lectures on spiritualism and morality are part of the daily routine in the schools. Religious songs and talks are also broadcast from the public address system fixed in the temple, so that it can be heard in any part of the village. There is a ban on eating non-vegetarian foods and smoking of cigarettes because these things presumably give rise to evil thoughts. Playing of film songs, watching of films or dances (*Chhayageet, Chitrahar*) on TV are also prohibited.

Life of women has also changed as a result of all these changes in the village. Wife beating and teasing of young women which were common features ten years ago, have totally disappeared. If any case of wife beating is reported, the man is given a public beating. Free from the habit of drinking, men now pay more attention to their family and children. Because of increased agricultural activity both men and women have to work much more than before; however the family life is happier and women and children are healthier. However the *Mahila Mandal* is yet to become an active women's group in the village.

The success of Ralegan Siddhi raises many questions. What are the critical inputs or factors in its success? Can it be replicated or multiplied at other places? Per capita investments in development projects implemented in Ralegan Siddhi over ten years (1975 to 1985) has been of the order of Rs.500 per capita per year. Of this, 11.7% was contributed by the village, 41.5% came in the form of government subsidies, 37% was contributed by the banks as short/long term loans most of which had already been repaid at the time of this study. As a result the annual per capita income in Ralegan had gone up from Rs. 270 in 1975 to Rs. 2257 in 1986, which amounts to 24% growth per year over ten years.

As a principle the people do not accept any financial assistance as donation. They insist that the money is given only as a loan which is to be paid back. There are cases where they have refused to accept moneys from charitable funding agencies and industrialists.

The Ralegan model is basically a self-help model. It is not the money (investments) alone or just the faithful implementation of government programmes that has made Ralegan's development an outstanding phenomenon. It has an advantage over others since there are no external catalytical inputs or agents which have to be withdrawn to test its sustaining power or analyse its multipliability.

The critical factors in Ralegan's success have been the people of Ralegan including the leadership of Anna Hazare.

Anna Hazare did receive assistance and support from various individuals and institutions from time to time. The Rural Welfare Board of Dorabji Tata Trust, Shri V. S. Page, former Chairmen of the Maharashtra Legislative Council; Balasaheb Bharde, former President to Khadi Gramodyog Sanghl Balasaheb Vikhe Patil, Member of Parliamentl Anil Kumar Lakhina, former Collector of Ahmednagar District; Navalbhai Firodia of Pune and Mrs. Leelatai Mulgaonkar of Tatas and many others interacted with Anna Hazare and the people of Ralegan, and made their contribution to the development of Ralegan Siddhi in different ways.

Success begets success. The bureaucracy saw that the government schemes are being successfully implemented in Ralegan showing 100% results. The bureaucracy also realized that they cannot "make any money" through corrupt practices there. Hence, they also contributed in making Ralegan a "showpiece" where they could demonstrate the success of their schemes. Many schemes were sanctioned to Ralegan out of turn. However this is not to deny that a large number of government officials from different departments at the *Taluka* and district levels as well as the *Gram Sevak* and *Talati* did get genuinely inspired and worked spiritedly for the implementation of various development projects in Ralegan.

When Anna was asked how he cut across the bureaucratic red tapism, he replied that he always brought pressure trom the top, either from the district level or at times from Bombay, to get the local bureaucracy "to fall in line".

Ralegan Siddhi has already started radiating its message of self-help to various villages in different parts of the country. Groups of people from over a hundred villages have visited Ralegan on their own initiative and taken the message from here to their respective villages. When such groups visit Ralegan they are taken around by any young worker in the village, be it the *Gram Sevak*, a teacher from the school or a member of the Village Youth Association. Anna Hazare's talk and personal discussions with them of course gives a sense of fulfillment. What the village people appreciate most is that development in Ralegan has been brought about by people like themselves with the help of Government schemes which can be available to them as well. Taking inspiration for self-help when these visitors go back to their respective villages, they do try to mobilize themselves for improvement in their social and economic life. The greatest advantage is that they do not have to look for a messiah in any individual or organization. In most cases their group visits have been followed by Anna Hazare himself paying a personal visit to these villages at their invitation. He has detailed discussions with the local youth and *Panchayat* members. In many of these villages programmes like ban on sale and consumption of alcohol and those of environmental conservation, like construction of checkdams and tree plantation have already started showing results.

The typical example of this contagious effect was observed by one of the authors in the village of Malshiras (in Purandar *Taluka* of Pune District). He was staying there for five years on a health education project. The village people and their youth association members had heard of Ralegan Siddhi through newspapers and television programmes. About thirty-five of them organized a visit to Ralegan in August 1987. After coming back from Ralegan, the members of the village *Panchayat* and Youth Association came together and adopted a ban on drinking and selling of liquor in the village. The five sellers of liquor were called to a meeting of the villagers and were told to "pack off".

Thus the ground was prepared for the visit of Anna Hazare. He came to the village in October 1987 and had a half day discussion with young workers. As a result, the village youths and *Panchayat* leadership felt inspired to take up many other development programmes. And ever since, the model of Ralegan has often been discussed in the village es well as in the meetings of the Village Youth Association.

To consolidate the multiplier effect, Ralegan has started training programmes of different durations (three days, fifteen days, three months and two years) for inspired and motivated young persons from different villages. A hostel for such trainees has been constructed to house such trainees and other students.

Ralegan Siddhi may well remain an island, like most other development experiments. But it has shown that if people decide to take up their own development through self-help and by integrating all sections of society, the united force of the people helped by motivated leadership has the capacity to transform the village. In the case of Ralegan, the bureaucracy and the political vested interests had fallen in line to share the glory of success, when they realized that they cannot make money through corruption in Ralegan. This may not be the case if many Ralegan' s spring up. But it may still create tremendous pressure on the system for change and a demand on the bureaucracy to "get off the people's backs".

Ralegan Before 1975

Ralegan Siddhi is located in the drought prone Parner Taluka of Ahmednagar district and is surrounded by small barren hills. The village is known by two names - Ralegan Siddhi and Ralegan Shindi. Some people say that the name Shindi has come from the '*Shindi*' plants which grew in abundance all around Ralegan long ago. While others prefer Siddhi because they believe that the name Siddhi came from some saints (*Siddhas* - the enlightened ones) who made Ralegan their abode over a hundred years ago. However, today Ralegan is better known as Anna Hazare's Ralegan.

Even before Anna started his work in Ralegan Siddhi in 1975, the village had earned a name in the neighbouring areas. It was well known as a source of illicit liquor. It was also known for goondaism and vandalism.

The old people recollect that Ralegan was not bad all through history. In fact, according to them the decline in the social and economic life of Ralegan came in their own lifetime. They also relate stories of Ralegan's glory. During the latter half of the 19th century to the first half of the 20th century, Ralegan was famous for its religious and God-fearing people. In 1950 a religious saint known as Sant Yadav Baba Kurhade came and settled down in this village. During Yadav Baba's lifetime, it is said that people from far away places used to come seeking an audience with him and to listen to his discourses.

Even after Yadav Baba's death, for many years Ralegan was like any other Indian village with simple people living in harmony with nature and lots of trees around. The people were not very rich but it is said that, there was enough to satisfy everyone's needs. Very old people of Ralegan do remember stories of forest and wild animals on the hills around the village. In due course the forests were destroyed and the village was caught in a cycle of recurring droughts. An uncertainty gripped agriculture and repeated crop failures made people diffident and fatalistic. Impoverishment of the villagers by recurrent droughts, goondaism of the vested interests and alcoholism had vitiated the social life to such an extent that no one from the neighbouring villages would marry one's daughter to an eligible bachelor from Ralegan.

Gradually, neglect of villages and destruction of nature to meet the growing needs of the urban population also took their toll on Ralegan Siddhi. Soil erosion, depleting water table and erratic rainfall dragged Ralegan into a perpetual drought cycle. Recurring droughts and degraded agriculture set into people's lives. It led to impoverishment of the people and degeneration of social life. One "enterprising" person from the village who found it difficult to support his family with the income from his land went to a neighbouring village and mastered the technique of distilling liquor.

His success attracted many others to this business. In due course, there were about 40 illicit distilling stills in the village. The clientele also grew from Ralegan as well as from the neighbouring villages. A large number of people from Ralegan got into habitual drinking. The worst sufferers of alcoholism in a village society are the women and children. In a male dominated society if the father is an alcoholic, the family gets disrupted and women and children have to pay the costs since all the decisions are still taken by the alcoholic male. Women in Ralegan used to get beaten by their alcoholic husbands for trivial reasons. The youth also started drinking and uncontrolled vandalism increased to the level that no young woman could dare to step out on the village streets after sunset. In the evening the village streets used to be full of drunkards roaming around. Gang fights were also quite frequent. The police had a 'happy' relation with a village of this kind. They could collect regular pay-offs from the liquor business as well as from those who were involved in the fights.

Except for the 35-40 families who were engaged in the business of illicit liquor, most other families were living in a state of absolute poverty. Persistent drought conditions and alcoholism had driven most of the people into heavy debts. Scarcity of fodder also made it difficult for the people to support milch and draught cattle. Large number of people used to go to work as daily wage labourers on drought relief works. Poor agricultural production and pressure of private money lenders to repay their debts had forced many people to migrate to other places in search of work.

Most of the people who went to the cities of Bombay, Pune or Ahmednagar in the 60's or early 70's were from the poorest families. They mostly worked as unskilled labourers or as coolies. At least one person from each *Harijan* family was working in a city in 1975. Some old villagers remember that for about two-thirds of the village households, the income from agriculture was not sufficient even to feed the family and at least a third of the households missed a meal almost every other day.

There was shortage of water in the village. However, the village sustained itself by meeting its minimum water requirements from one or two wells. Living under these conditions of insufficient food, alcoholic males and shortage of drinking water, it is not difficult to imagine the health status of the people.

Beside other diseases, people also remember that incidence of guinea-worm infection was very common. The nearest medical service available was at Shirur or Parner, both about 14 kms away from the village. Infant and child mortality were so high that there was a separate cremation ground for them.

School education was totally neglected by the people of Ralegan. Till 1965 there was only one classroom for a primary school. In I 965 one more classroom was added and the school was later extended upto the 7th standard. There were hardly any girls studying beyond the 4th standard. Very few boys went to Shirur or Parner to pursue their studies beyond the 7th standard. There was only one state transport bus for going to Shirur or Parner schools. Thus transport also became an inhibiting factor for students to pursue their studies, in addition to the family and social life in the village which was far from congenial for children to study properly.

The social life of the village was also plagued by the practice of untouchability and caste discrimination. There was no separate well for the *harijans*, and the upper castes would not allow the *harijans* to draw water directly from the common well. They had to wait tor someone from the upper castes to draw water and pour it into their vessels from a distance. *Harijans* had to sit in a separate row in every community lunch and they were served food the last.

Harijans had heen given about 60 acres of land during the British rule. They did not have resources to develop and cultivate these lands. In 1973, seventeen *harijan* families came together and took a loan of Rs. 22,500/- from the Ahmednagar District Co-operative Bank for digging a common well to irrigate their fields. The well was dug but it yielded insufficient water. Distribution of water and repayment of loans could not be managed properly and as a result these households sank deeper into debt; the bank threatened to recover the dues by auctioning their lands.

There was no co-operative spirit in the village and no community feeling. The village *Panchayat* leadership had no role except to appropriate every Government scheme for personal benefit. The ration shop was owned by one such leader, and the supplies were often sold in the black market. At every village function, whether it was a marriage ceremony or a religious function, celebrations were invariably marred by hooliganism. Almost every week there was a police case filed from the village on account of thefts of the harvested crops from the house, fights over loans, lands or on eve-teasing. Even the relations among Marathas (land holding caste) were far from harmonious. There was competition and ego clashes used to occur on issues like who spent more on his son's or daughter's wedding or during the village feasts during the festivals.

Once a year the village *jatra* is held at Padmavati temple in the village. Goats were offered to the deity and sacrificed at the temple. This was followed by feasts where mutton and liquor were served. Fights over petty reasons were very common on such occasions. Even on the *Bail Pola* day there used to be clashes on the question of which bullocks entered the village first to head the procession of decorated bullocks. Thus non-issues were made into prestige matters by the powerful people just to satisfy their egos. But, these village leaders never bothered to do anything that would benefit the people.

In 1972, when severe drought struck most parts of Maharashtra, various Tata Trusts and Tata Companies formed the "Tata Relief Committee". This committee started working in six villages of Parner *Taluka*. The Tata Relief Committee undertook the work of reaching drinking water to the villages by tankers and also took up the construction of check-dams under "food for work" program in Ralegan Siddhi and in other villages. This programme was supported by food grains from the Catholic Relief Society. After the drought, the Rural Welfare Board of Dorabji Tata Trust continued with various programmes like provision of medical relief and deepening of wells in addition to construction of check-dams for water conservation.

Thus, when Anna Hazare entered the scene in 1975, he was presented with a totally hopeless social and economic situation and irresponsible village leadership. The only soothing factor was the relief work started by Mr. Ashok Bedarkar, a young and enthusiastic social scientist, who was the Project Officer of the Dorabji Tata Trust.

The Development Process

Rural development has been a very popular theme in the last two decades. A large number of young persons with university degrees went into the villages and set up rural development experiments. Hundreds of books have been written during this period critically examining various approaches, expounding different models and setting numerous standards of evaluation. Self-help and community participation have been the most talked about but rarely achieved goals of rural development experiments.

When Anna Hazare started working in Ralegan Siddhi, he did not have any model before him. The entire course of development in Ralegan was charted out by the people themselves. Local ingenuity, people's grasp and understanding about the roots of the problems, their openness in accepting ideas from all sources, Anna's honesty and hard

taskmaster attitude and above all, the collective response in taking up and implementing various schemes by the people, brought about the overall transformation. The process of transformation in Ralegan therefore cannot be put into the frame of any textbook model of development.

The Gandhian dictum is that change should begin at the individual level. If the individuals change the village will change; and if the villages are changed, the country will be changed. This can be clearly observed in the development approach followed in case of Ralegan Siddhi. Stress on personal morality, abstaining from alcohol, cigarettes and from non-vegetarian foods are essential components of a personal code of conduct imposed in Ralegan.

These are in fact considered the necessary conditions of social development too. Personal morality of course is not restricted to teetotalism. It has been linked to a broader vision of social morality encompassing social equality and egalitarian distribution of the benefits of growth. Divergence from alcoholism was considered to be a basic step towards creating a new sense of social responsibility and for the growth of developmental spirit. The concept of personal morality here has been drawn chiefly from Hindu religion. It is a temple where oath for giving up drinking was taken. It is a temple where all the disputes are settled because people believe that no one would tell a lie sitting in the temple. Moral education in the school includes reading of scriptures and chanting of Bhajans. Religious discourses, quotations from religious saints and playing of bhajans are a regular morning routine in the temple.

Normally, religious personal morality does not go beyond one's personal life. If it does, it takes the form of charity or philanthropy. Therefore, the person can continue to build up his wealth and amass riches by exploiting others and still feel self-righteous by doing some charity. In Ralegan, however, personal morality and social morality have been beautifully inter-linked for laying the foundation of a new social order. Practice of untouchability and discrimination on the basis of caste or wealth have been totally banished from the social life. In the economic development programmes, socialisation of costs and socialisation of surpluses are two outstanding features. In the implementation of every project utilities, planting of trees or deepening of wells, *Shramadaan* is always an important component. The *Shramadaan* phenomenon achieves two purposes. Firstly it socialises the cost of the project and secondly people develop a sense of belonging to the project because of their contribution in creating it and therefore they maintain it well. *Shramadaan* reduced initial costs and (therefore) also the burden of bank loans to be repaid. Hence the surplus starts accruing much faster The surpluses are also socialised by an egalitarian distribution mechanism wherein 25% of the surplus generated goes towards a village fund from which other community benefit schemes are implemented. The principle followed is that for distribution of benefit the village comes first and then the individual. Therefore almost all the projects implemented in the village are group benefit projects. The village takes care that all the village households are covered by some group benefit schemes as far as possible, so that every one is also directly benefited in addition to receiving indirect benefits from the community projects. Special attention has been paid to the development of the deprived sections of the society, so that the inequality gap is reduced. It is a remarkable example of social morality that better-off farmers were involved in cultivating the *harijan* lands to help them come out of the debt trap. Hence, in spite of rapid economic development, disparities within Ralegan have decreased instead of getting widened.

Though people of Ralegan deserved the credit duly attributed to them by Anna Hazare himself, the role of leadership in Ralegan's success should not be understated. Today, Anna has become a charismatic leader. Any scheme he suggests are generally given full support by the bureaucracy and politicians. The people of Ralegan however had accepted Anna's leadership much before he got recognised in outside circles.

Anna did not have any ancestry or his own past to act as a pedestal to launch into his social life. He did not go to the people with a political ideology like a political activist or with promises of economic benefits like a trade-unionist. He did not mobilise people by distributing personal favours through his influence with people in power. The only term that can charactcrise Anna's leadership is "moral leadership".

Ralegan's example has shown that moral leadcrship still works with the people even 40 years after Mahatma Gandhi's death. Sacrifice has always been highly valued in Hindu philosophy. Sacrifice still establishes the moral authority of a person.

Renunciation of worldly desires and aspirations has been considered the only way to achieve *moksha* in the Hindu scriptures. Anna's giving up to his self-interest, money, land, property and family attachments raised his stature above everyone else in the village. People's faith that whatever he says or does is in pcople's interest has made him almost a saint. Anna's not getting married also added to his moral appeal and strength. The spending of all his gratuity money for the village temple also laid the foundation of his moral leadership. As soon as he could establish that he sacrificed his self interest for the common good, his leadership also got established. His opponents could not stand up to him. Moral leadership also has an advantage that it brings out the best from the ordinary people. The moral leadership of Anna has thus helped in the moral development of Ralegan Siddhi.

Over the years Anna has tried to build a second line of leadership in the village. He has also started training programmes for young workers from different villages. He insists that as far as possible these workers should remain unmarried (of late he has softened his stand on this condition). To ensure that worker's sustenance should not in any way be linked to the implementation of the project, Anna is arranging that a fixed deposit of around 40,000 to 50,000 rupees would be kept in the name of that selfless worker who would then devote himself fully for the village development work. In this way an effort has been made to have sacrifice and morality built into the leadership role.

The people of Ralegan are no dumb followers of Anna. Every new scheme is thoroughly discussed in village meetings. Pros and cons are considered. Plan of implementation and code of conduct are decided upon. A separate committee is selected by the people to look after the implementation of each program. Involvement of people in every aspect of the program is exemplary. The local *Gram Sevak, Talati,* school teacher and youths are seen explaining details of various programmes to the visitors.

Development with Equity

Unless conscious and painstaking efforts are made, all development leads to increasing disparities. So much so that in India, planned development seems to have planned for higher growth of inequalities. Poverty in Indian society has existed as a comprehensive package. The deprived section is deprived in all aspects: social, economic, political, cultural, information, knowledge, education, skills, health or even access to health care, initiative, self-confidence, leadership ...many more things may be added to this list. This inequity in development is well-illustrated by looking at a typical government program or new technology for rural areas. The upper strata will get to know of it first. They will show the initiative, enterprise and the confidence to take it up. They will implement it well and reap the benefits.

In contrast the programs specially meant for the poor are either diverted by the bureaucracy in collusion with the rural leadership to benefit the rich or remain only on paper. The money allocated for these progams is used elsewhere or is allowed to lapse. Because of these reasons the poor have lost faith in Government programs and they have not been able to develop any stakes in development activities taken up even at the village level.

In Ralegan Siddhi the people of Ralegan made sure that the first benefits of development reach the poor. They have succeeded in breaking the age old barriers and consequently the poor too have started having a stake in the development of Ralegan. This process has resulted in participation of the poor with new energies. Release of these energies has contributed to rapid and integrated development of Ralegan Siddhi.

According to a survey of Ralegan taken by its *Gram Sevak* in 1986, there were 41 families of *dalits* living in the village. Out of them were 17 *Mahars,* 15 *Chambhars,* 2 *Matangs,* I *Nhavi,* 1 *Bharhadi* and 5 were *Sutar* families. Five of these families were landless. *Mahars, Chambars* and *Matangs* are the three castes which come lowest on the Hindu caste ladder. Untouchability in many forms did exist in Ralegan. These people were not allowed inside the temple. They were given water from the well but not allowed to draw water from the well on their own. They were not allowed to participate in community functions and marriages. During community lunches they had to sit separately and were served the last.

At Anna Hazare's initiative the people of Ralegan decided to alleviate these disparities at both the social and economic levels. The dalits now participate in all the social functions. Their marriages are held as part of community marriage program together with those of other castes. As members of the *Tarun Mandal, Mahila Mandal* and *Gram panchayat* the *harijans* are even part of the team cooking or serving food in community lunches, even to the higher caste people. Once the *Satyanarayanpooja* in a local temple was performed by a local. These activities have helped in breaking the social barriers between *dalits* and other castes.

In 1972 eleven *dalit* families had jointly borrowed Rs. 22,500/ from the Ahmednagar Bank for bringing their 32 acres of land under irrigation. They did dig a well and lay a pipeline to their fields with this money but a few years later, because of some discord amongst themselves the electricity bills were not paid and repayment schedule of the bank loan was also not followed. As a result, the bank decided to recover the arrears (loan and interest totalling about Rs. 75,000) by auctioning the land. Anna Hazare intervened at this point and on his suggestion the *Tarun Mandal* took the responsibility of cultivating the land on lease for 10 years and pay back the loans. The bank officials also agreed to allow a grace period. The *Tarun Mandal* paid off the loans in just three years by collective farming on these lands. Later some of these lands were brought under farm-forestry by planting Subabul (Lucena) trees which yielded fodder and fire-wood. During the lease period the dalit owners got 25% of the produce and after the lease was over the lands were handed back to the original owners.

For all other economic programs the people from the oppressed castes were chosen to be the first beneficiaries. Twenty-five women got cows or goats with Government subsidy and bank loans and became members of the cooperative society. *Dalit* wells were repaired/ deepened with Government grant and a co-operative society was registered for sharing of water. A community centre with an electric connection was built, landless families were given land (5 acres each) and 9 houses were constructed with a NREP (National Rural Employment Program) grant. Like in any other village in India, *dalit* houses in Ralegan also were on the outskirts of the village. The new houses were built next to the village temple. The village people also contributed to construction of these houses by way of *Shramadaan*. All these houses have a lighting connection and smokeless *chulhas*. *Dalits* have also benefited by way of subsidies and loans for sewing machines, irrigation pumps, *gobar* gas plants, common toilets and bathrooms, free books, notebooks and uniforms for the school children. Seventeen families are members of the Krishna Lift Irrigation Schemes.

The only barber in the village used to hire out for wage labour to supplement income from the traditional occupation. He received training in running a poultry farm and with a bank loan of Rs. 9,000 he was able to start a poultry farm as an additional source of income.

The carpenter families are also farmers. They have been able to improve their agriculture. Three of them got loans for buying cows, one of them dug a well and bought a pumpset with assistance from the bank for irrigating his fields. One of these families opened a grocery shop, also with bank assistance.

During the ten year period i.e. from 1976 to 1986, the Social Welfare Department had spent Rs. 7.93 lakh and the *Panchayat Samitis* had spent Rs. 73,000 under IRDP (Integrated Rural Development Program) grant on program of economic advancement of *Dalit* families in Ralegan Siddhi.

However, more significant than the amount of money spent is the spirit of integration that thc people of Ralegan have demonstrated. They have shown that development with equity is real development and that it is also possible to accomplish this within a short span of 10 years.

Watershed Development - Key to Economic Growth

Geographically, Ralegan is surrounded by small hillocks on the north-east and on the southern sides. The slopes of these hills on the eastern side give rise to the main run-off water stream during the rainy season. The geographical area (982 ha.) of Ralegan can be roughly divided into four watershed zones. Since the land is undulating most of the landholdings are small.

The village is located in a drought prone (rain-shadow) zone with erratic rainfall between 200 mm and 850 mm per year. According to the 1971 census only 55 acres of land were irrigated. During that period most of the rainwater was wasted as run-off also taking the valuable top soil with it and rendering the cultivable lands poorer in productivity.

The older generation of Ralegan does recollect existence of a lot of green hushy vegetation on the hill slopes. By the seventies however, all of it had disappeared and there were no soil conservation measures undertaken. The villagers used to construct small mud *bandharas* across the *nullahs* to divert the water to irrigate their fields. But there was no water-harvesting effort as such. Most of the wells used to be dry by the month of December or January. Some of the wells however did though barely, satisty the requirements of drinking water.

In the year 1972 like most parts of Maharashtra, Ralegan experienced the worst drought in living memory, when almost every able bodied person in the village worked on relief works. It was during this year that the Tata Relief Committee (TRC) also started relief work in 6 villages of Parner *Taluka,* including Ralegan. The work was later extended to include five more villages. In 1972 the TRC constructed a community well in the village and also started constructing check-dams with assistance from the Catholic Relief Society under its "Food for Work" program. In all 11 checkdams were constructed in the village under this program.

In 1975 a percolation tank was sanctioned by the government in the eastern watershed area with a storage capacity of 114.2 lakh cubic feet of water. Construction of tank did create over 1 lakh mandays of work over a period of one and a half years. However the basic objective of water harvesting was not achieved since all the accumulated water used to rapidly seep away through the previous base of the bund (embankment wall).

It was in 1975 that Anna Hazare started his work in the village. Realizing the importance of water harvesting he pleaded with the district authorities about the need to undertake repairs of the percolation tank built at a cost of Rs. 4.35 lakh. After a lot of effort the Zilla Parishad agreed and in 1983-84 the massive repair work of providing impervious foundation to the tank was completed costing another Rs. 3.9 lakhs. The villagers could see the results immediately as the seven wells in the downstream got charged giving enough water even during the summer.

Under Anna Hazare's leadership the people of Ralegan had started participating in the implementation of every village level development program through *Shramadaan*. Anna himself, and his *Tarun Mandal* volunteers supervised every program to ensure that quality of work and construction standards were maintained so that maximum possible benefits were achieved with minimum wastage. Seeing this enthusiasm of the people of Ralegan, Shri Anil

Lakhina, the then Collector of Ahmednagar district announced COWDEP (Comprehensive Wasteland Development Program) for Ralegan and the Agriculture Department also selected Ralegan for *Krishi Pandhari* (Farm training and visits) scheme as a corollary of the COWDEP. Soil Conservation and the Social Forestry Departnents also joined in to strengthen the soil conservation and watershed development efforts.

The strategy adopted was of checking the run-off water by contour bounding, constructing check-dams so as to hold the water within the watershed area. Land shaping and land grading were strengthened by massive tree plantation and pasture development program. About 3,00,000 trees were planted by 1986, covering an area of about 102hectares to provide fodder and meet the fuel requirements of the village.

Having planted trees on the roadside, on bunds of check-dams, on boundaries of individual fields, on community lands and wastelands in the village, the tree plantation has now extended to the barren hills which surround Ralegan village. This massive drive of tree plantation has earned Anna Hazare the national award of Indira Priyadarshini *Vrikshamitra*.

Ralegan has successfully experimented with the idea of "social fencing" for protection of trees. Having understood the critical importance of trees for getting out of the cycle of environmental degradation and drought the village people adopted a ban on open grazing of cattle. A couple of households resisted and flouted the ban. Anna Hazare along with some members of the *Tarun Mandal* commenced a 'fast' and as a result even these deviant families submitted to the collective will of the people.

Raising of nurseries has been taken up in a decentralized manner taking advantage of government schemes wherever possible. These water conservation and environmental regeneration programs have made Ralegan Siddhi an oasis in the drought prone *taluka* of Parner. But the people of Ralegan are not insensitive to the existing disparities.

Utilization of Harvested Water

Anna Hazare often says that it is not the water in fields that brings true development, rather it is water in the eyes (i.e. compassion for the fellow beings) that brings real development. Therefore the emphasis was on distribution of benefits especially in such a way that the poorest are chosen as the first beneficiaries. Water resources created by community effort were therefore shared by the people through water supply co-operatives. Five such societies have been formed to extend the benefits of irrigation to the maximum number of people. According to a rough count by the *Gram Sevak* in 1988 there were 40 new wells dug to reap the benefits of water harvesting. The total area irrigated by well water has gone up to 700 acres. By 1991 there were 87 private and 7 community wells in Ralegan.

To supplement this effort a lift irrigation scheme was taken up in 1986 under which water from the nearby Kukdi Canal was lifted to bring another 500 acres under irrigation benefiting 103 farmers. For all these irrigation schemes the labour component was provided by the beneficiaries in the form of *Shramadaan* and the Bank of Maharashtra extended a helping hand by providing loans. Wherever possible the benefit of subsidy under various Government schemes was also taken.

Drinking Water

Prior to the watershed development program there were only two wells which used to sustain the village during the summer months. People had to walk 2-3 Kms to fetch water. Even in the worst drought however, as one well in the village never dried up, drinking water was never supplied to the village by tankers.

By 1986 there were eight bore wells installed in the village. A motor pump on one of these bore wells supplies piped water to different clusters of houses by rotation. Another motor on a bore well near Padmavati temple supplies piped water to the boys' hostel. No one has to walk a long distance anymore for water and there is no crowding for drinking water.

Water Management

Ralegan has also experimented with drip and bi-valve irrigation in a big way. Papaya, lemon and chillies have been planted on a plot of 80 acres entirely irrigated by the drip irrigation system. People who have dug private wells in their fields have been persuaded not to raise water-intensive cash crops like sugarcane. However groundnut and onion have been allowed to some extent. When the villages around Ralegan were facing acute shortage of fodder, the people of Ralegan demonstrated a unique sense of social commitment by producing more fodder instead of taking cash crops and supplying it to neighhouring villages at prices lower than the market rates.

Within Ralegan all those families who have benefited from extension of irrigation contribute 25% of their increased incomes to other community based projects so that the benefits are shared. The Ralegan people have also monetarily contributed towards rehahilitation of those farmers who were divested of their lands for construction of the Kukdi canal as well as the dam which feeds the canal, once again demonstrating the human face of development.

Economic Development

For economic development, the first program taken up in Ralegan was that of environment regeneration. Harvesting of all the rainwater within the boundaries of Ralegan was undertaken through watershed development i.e. by percolation tank, contour bundling, construction of check-dams (*nullah* bundings) and large scale tree plantation. These programs revitalised the existing well in the village. Many new wells were dug and utilization of water was regulated through six co-operative irrigation societies. As a result, about 700 acres of land were brought under irrigation. In addition, another 500 acres were brought under irrigation by a lift irrigation scheme from the Kukdi Canal. The area under irrigation is now being expanded further by using drip irrigation techniques. Water from two wells now suffices to irrigate 100 acres of land by drip irrigation, which is five times the area that would have been irrigated by traditional methods.

To take full advantage of extension of irrigation, help was taken of the extension of the State Agriculture Department. Ralegan farmers received help and guidance under the *Krishi Pandhari* scheme in which the agricultural extension officers pay visits to individual farms and provide guidance and training to the farmers in the field itself.

The farmers started growing high yield varieties of crop and the cropping pattern of the village also changed.

Kharif: In 1975-76, 240 hectares were under rainfed *Bajra* with only 20 hectares of irrigated *Bajra*. In 1985-86 rainfed *Bajra* was grown only in 60 hectares whereas 150 hectares were put under high yield *Bajra* with assured irrigation. Green vegetables were grown only in two hectares in 1975-76. Whereas during 1985-86, 60 hectares were used for growing vegetables. These vegetables found ready markets in Pune and Bombay. There was not much change in the area of oilseeds production. However, in 1985-86, irrigation was extended to 15 more hectares of land under oilseed crops thus increasing the oilseed production.

Rabi: In 1975-76 rainfed *Jowar* was grown in 320 hectares and *Jowar* in 50 hectares was irrigated whereas in 1985-86 *Jowar* with irrigation was grown in 250 hectares whereas rainfed *Jowar* was grown only in 90 hectares. During the same period rainfed wheat decreased from 12 hectares to 7 hectares and irrigated area under wheat grew from 1 hectare to 23 hectares. For oilseeds the irrigated area grew from nil to 17 hectares and rainfed crop area declined from 30 hectares to 10 hectares. Vegetable production during *Rabi* period particularly received a boost, increasing from 3 hectares to 25 hectares.

As a result of these changes total agricultural production went up from 294.3 tonnes in 1975-76 to 1386.2 tonnes in 1985-86. At current prices it meant an increase from Rs. 3.46 lakh to Rs. 31.73 lakh i.e. 4.7fold increase in quantity and a 9-fold increase in value.

Milk Production

As a secondary occupation, milk production was promoted in Ralegan. Purchase of new cattle and improvement of the existing breed with the help of artificial insemination and timely guidance and assistance by the veterinary doctor has resulted in an improvement in the cattle stock. The milk production has also increased. Crossbred cows are replacing the local ones which give a low milk yield. The number of milch cattle has also been growing. In 1987 there were 574 milch cattle (including 65 cross-bred cows) as compared to 255 in 1981. Around 350 litres of milk were collected per day and sent to a co-operative dairy in Ahmednagar. Some milk is also given to *Balwadi* children in Ralegan and in Pimpalner, a neighbouring village under the child nutrition program sponsored by the *Zilla Parishad*.

From the surplus generated, the milk society bought a mini-truck and a thresher. The mini-truck besides transporting milk to Ahmednagar is also used for taking vegetahles and other produce directly to the market, thus eliminating intermediate agents. The thresher is rented out to the farmers during the harvesting season.

Grain Bank

The village also runs a grain bank, collecting small contributions from farmers having surplus production. This ensures subsidized supply of foodgrains to the farmers having deficient production. The grain bank also helps in preventing distress sale of grain at a low price at the time of harvest and purchase at a higher price from the market during the lean period before the next crop. In 1975-76 only 20 guintals of foodgrain were collected during the year whereas this collection increased to 40 quintals in 1985-86.

Secondary occupations like poultry farming were also encouraged, but with limited success. Out of the 10 persons who received training only one person was actually running a poultry successfully. Traditional artisans were assisted by subsidies and bank loans to improve the income generating capacity of their traditional occupations. There has been visible improvement in their living standards too.

Another factor that has contributed substantially to the increase in the living standards of Ralegan people has been the repatriation of large incomes from the people who have been able to find better jobs in larger numbers because of better educational qualifications/ standards. In 1975-76 only 20 persons were in jobs with an average earning of Rs. 200 per month whereas in 1985-86. Over 90 persons were earning an average of Rs. 1000 p.m. in their city jobs.

Like most villagers do, the people of Ralegan are also seen to have invested their initial increase in income into improving their agricultural base. Buying a pump, PVC pipeline for irrigation, a pair of bullocks, cross-bred cows come first. Improvement in nutrition, education of children and seeking immediate treatment of ailment has developed simultaneous to the growth of incomes. Improvement in houses comes next. Initially only 2-3 households who had some of their earning members in the city undertook renovation of their house. Later, one could see many more new houses being constructed.

A stage is now set for development of secondary job opportunities through industrialization in the village so that the educated and trained youth can find gainful employment in the village itself instead of migrating to urban slums. All the traditional occupations have been helped to grow with financial assistance from banks. People have been trained in some new trades like sewing and raising of poultry. A *Khadi* unit is also being started with 25 six-spindle *charkhas* and 5 handlooms. A *masala* pounding and packing unit is also being planned. Chillies have been planted in 80 acres of land to provide raw material for this unit. The village is moving in the direction of becoming self-sufficient along Gandhian lines, where all the basic needs of the village population will be met from the production units in the village itself. Agro-based processing industries will lay the foundation of industrialisation in Ralegan and Anna Hazare proclaims that nothing except common salt will have to be bought from outside to satisfy the basic needs of the people of Ralegan.

Social Development

Economic advancement alone may not improve the quality of life. On the contrary it may also lead to social and cultural degradation. Symptoms of this degeneration may show up in many forms, like terrorism, juvenile and organized crime, drug addiction, vulgar display of riches and total neglect and antipathy towards the poor. Any system that supports or even tolerates gross disparities is both inhuman and immoral. Such a system cannot bring about progress of human society.

Often the new-rich in the cities and many of the new professional class are heard blaming the poor themselves for their poverty. The poor are branded as lazy, illiterate, ignorant and inefficient. Often the poor also internalise this perception about themselves and develop a low self-image with the result that consequences of poverty are seen as causes of poverty.

When the people of Ralegan under the leadership of Anna Hazare decided to throw off these burdens from their backs and chart a new path, it was a difficult and deep struggle for social change at two simultaneous levels, personal as well as the community. Changes at the individual level are essential for societal level changes to be meaningful. Social morality is farcical if the people at an individual level, are authoritarian, casteist, communal or sexist. However, social pressure often helps in bringing about conformity to normative behaviour at the individual level.

Campaign against Alcoholism

In Ralegan, Anna saw that the village temple was in a dilapidated condition. Even some of the wooden pillars and beams had been pulled out and burned as firewood in the liquor stills. This temple had been constructed years ago in the name of Yadav Baba, a saint who preached and also breathed his last in Ralegan Siddhi. Yadav Baba has almost been looked upon as a village deity. Anna started the work of reconstruction of the village temple with Rs. 20,000 of his provident fund and gratuity. This act of Anna moved the villagers. People came forward and offered contributions in cash and kind to the tune of Rs. 90,000. A youth group was formed to supervise the construction work.

Whenever old and young people gathered in the temple, Anna used to tell them about the need to have a ban on liquor in the village and to close down the liquor stills if the village had to make any progress. Finally, one day a village meeting was held in the temple and it was decided to impose a total ban on making, selling and drinking of liquor. The villagers took an oath in the name of Yadav Baba and also decided on a code of discipline to implement it. The person who started the first liquor still was also the first to close down his business. Even today one sees him in the temple and, though older to Anna Hazare, he touches Anna's feet.

Implementation of total ban on sale and consumption of liquor was not an easy task. All those involved in making and selling of liquor were helped to find alternative vocations. The habitual drunkards were persuaded, warned and the incorrigible ones were given a public beating. Still, there were some known goondas who defied the village unity. After a few instances of public punishments the village remained free of alcoholism. Gradually the opposition died out and Anna's selfless moral Ieadership rose to mobilize the entire village.

After the people of Ralegan took an oath in front of the village temple to implement the ban on sale and consumption of alcohol, the change was achieved in three stages - some people gave up drinking alcohol after realizing the evil effects of excessive drinking, some of them required heavy persuasion and the third category yielded under social pressure when some of them were given physical punishment in public. After the full achievement of this campaign the village youth started fighting the other social evils.

Collective Marriages

Most rural poor get into a debt-trap as they have to incur heavy expenses at the time of the marriage of their son or daughter. It is an undesirable practice but has almost become a social obligation. Ralegan's people have started celebrating the marriages collectively. The feast is held together where the expenses are further reduced by the *Tarun Mandal* taking the responsibility of cooking and serving the food. The vessels, the Loud-speaker system, the *mandap* and the decorations have also been bought by the *Tarun Mandal* members belonging to the oppressed castes. From 1976 to 1986, four hundred and twenty four marriages have been held under this system.

Banishing Dowry

The evil practice of dowry given at the time of marriage is well known even to the village people. But this evil cannot be banished by individual action. Ralegan people do not accept any dowry at the time of their son's marriage. However, they cannot extend the same rule in the case of daughters of Ralegan i.e. no dowry will be given in their daughter's marriage. Till such consciousness to banish dowry reaches other villages it is bound to remain only a one-sided affair for the people of Ralegan.

Untouchability

The people of Ralegan have largely succeeded in eradicating social discrimination on the basis of caste. The dalits have been integrated into the social and economic life of the village. Obviously the initiative for this had to come from the upper castes and the leadership of the *Tarun Mandal*. The people of all castes, however responded very well to this process of social integration.

Fighting Superstitions

Goddess Padmavati is the village deity of Ralegan. During the annual village festival of goddess Padmavati, the people used to bring goats to the Padmavati temple for sacrifice. After the sacrificial killing of the goat and ritual of offering it to the goddess the people had a feast at their homes with meat and alcohol freely served to relatives and other guests. During the pooja rituals some persons would start dancing vigorously pretending that they were possessed by the goddess. The villagers would ask questions about their problems and seek remedies from these persons (often called *devarshis*) supposedly blessed with divine powers. This entire drama gave rise to many superstitious practices. People used to trust the *tantra-mantra* or the ash given by this person even for treatment of well-known infectious diseases. These practices were not peculiar to Ralegan Siddhi but the people of Ralegan, especially the *Tarun Mandal*, decided to put an end to it.

As a first step they told the people that if sacrificing a goat and offering it to the goddess pleased her then why should the sacrificial goat be taken home for a feast, let it remain with the goddess to make her happier. As a result, the practice of sacrificing animals at the temple stopped. Secondly when some people got "possessed" by the goddess and started dancing, the one who started first was beaten up by the *Tarun Mandal* members. He immediately started behaving normally; since that day no one in the village has ever got possessed by the goddess! Exposure of these practices has brought about a dramatic change in the beliefs of the people of Ralegan.

The people contributed their voluntary labour for the implementation of every project of community or group benefit. This has resulted in socialisation of costs along with the socialisation of benefits. From the benefits, every beneficiary contributed 10-25% of the surplus to the community fund from which many other schemes of common benefit were undertaken.

As a result, a sense of personal involvement and attachment has developed among the people for all community assets. Therefore, people take care of such assets. whether these are common toilets, water taps, the hostel building or the fruit bearing trees on common lands.

A sense of social obligation and sharing of benefits has also been built into every program. This consciousness has been demonstrated by the people of Ralegan in the form of running the grain bank, self-imposed restriction on growing water intensive cash crops, growing fodder and supplying it to neighbouring villages, helping oppressed caste families to get out of their debt trap and contributing towards the resettlement of people affected by the Kukdi Canal construction.

Nyaya Panchayat

Squabbles over sharing of water, straying of cattle into other's fields for grazing, and land disputes are very common in villages. Usually, these fights result in people filing complaints with the police and spending a lot of money in bribing the police or paying the lawyers. The people in Ralegan resolved that all such disputes would be settled at the *Gram Panchayat* level where the *Gram Panchayat* acted as a *Nyaya Panchayat*. As a result of increased social awareness and deeper community feeling, disputes are rare and all disputes have been amicably settled at the village level itself. From 1976-1986 not a single police case had been filed from this village at the police station.

Democratic Functioning

Collective decision making and election by consensus are the basic principles of democratic functioning in Ralegan. All public offices in *Gram Panchayat* or village co-operatives are considered as offices of responsibility and not as opportunities for gaining power and making money. Hence all the elections to the village level bodies are held in the *Gram Sabha* and as far as possible, by consensus. This practice has put an end to political factionalism that has vitiated the public life in almost every other village.

Even at the time of Assembly and Parliamentary elections the *Gram Sabha* holds a meeting to discuss the merits and demerits of each candidate as well as of their parties. These are discussed and then "whom to vote for" decided at the individual level. The usual campaigning by shouting through loudspeakers, taking out processions, etc, is not encouraged.

Women's Status

The women were asked in an informal group meeting as to what Ralegan's development has meant to them i.e. how have their lives changed. They replied, "earlier the men used to drink, waste their money and at home the women and children did not even have enough for their basic needs; they had to go hungry. Besides, the women were harassed both at home and outside. At home they were shouted at, beaten and reprimanded for trivialities. The men were drunkards, paid no attention to agricultural or domestic chores and used to pick fights and create scenes on the streets. We had to work hard at home, in the fields and take care of our drunkard husbands as well".

As a result of the developments that have taken place in Ralegan, their drugdgery has reduced. Water sources close to their house, gobar gas plants and smokeless chulhas have made their life easier though they are still found to be working much more than the menfolk. Their workload has to some extent, increased due to larger number of milch cattle to be looked after. But now the men are also taking greater responsibility in looking after the agricultural operations and at times even the children. Construction of public latrines and bathrooms has also been a great relief to women.

Many more girls are now going to school, and even seeking higher education. In 1971 only 12.33% of the girls were literate. In 1981 this figure went up to 24.24%. Literacy figures were not available for 1986 but in 1986-87 there were 200 girl students in Ralegan schools and 2 girls were doing the Diploma in Education and 4 others were studying in the twelfth standard in colleges outside Ralegan.

Due to increased social consciousness and improved economic conditions, health problems of women were now better taken care of. A case of wife battering was reported to the *Tarun Mandal* by the neighbours; the husband was pulled up and publicly admonished.

There is a *Mahila Mandal* in the village registered with the Charity Commissioner though an active women's group has still to emerge. Women do not, as yet, participate in the decision making at the *Gram*

Sabha level or in any other program. *Tarun Mandal* members and Anna Hazare himself have expressed the desire that some catalysts (women activists) are required to mobilize and activise the women of Ralegan.

Educational Development

Education is considered a necessary input for development. But the educational system in our country has always been biased against the poor. For centuries it ensured that women and *shudras* were kept away from its benefits and it helped the upper castes to maintain their dominant position. Today it helps the urban elites in maintaining their control over power in every sphere of the country and peoples' lives. The educational standards in rural schools are so poor that schooling only adds to the handicap that the youth from rural areas already have due to lack of exposure, poor communication skills and to add to it all, the English language. These conditions are so discriminatory against the poor that it only ensures that they can never break through the social and economic hierarchy in spite of small palliatives like reservations in jobs.

In Ralegan Siddhi the primary school (upto 4th std) was started as early as in 1932 understandably with one teacher and one room. India gained Independence and two Five Year Plans went by with the Second Plan specially acclaimed for its high success (11% growth rate). But even till 1962, for Ralegan primary school it was still the same dilapidated room with one teacher.

It was in 1962 that the villagers added one more room to the school by *shramadaan*. In spite of these conditions, in 1971 out of the total population of 1209, 30.43% (72 women and 290) men were literate. Many boys went to nearby towns viz. Shirur and Parner to continue their education, but rarely did a girl. The drop-out rate was high, more so for girls, for obvious socio-economic and cultural reasons.

Under Anna Hazare's leadership the people of Ralegan decided to break away from the vicious circle and use education as a meaningful input into integrated development. The *Tarun Mandal* started a *balwadi* in 1976 so that the children get an early start. They also started paying attention to the functioning of the primary school.

Soon they realized that the school was not providing any education to the children. They informed the *Zilla Parishad* (which runs the school) that the village had decided to close down the government school and run an alternative school on its own. The *Zilla Parishad* authorities realized the gravity of the threat - that this move on the part of villagers might rock their entire structure. They immediately transferred all the teachers and sent for the best teachers from all over the district and instructed them to work in co-operation with the *Tarun Mandal* and Anna Hazare. Under constant vigilance of the people of Ralegan, the primary school is now working very well.

The people also decided to start a high school in the village itself to ensure proper education to the village children during the formative years and also that more girls could also avail of education. A local body under the name of Sant Yadav Baba Shikshan Prasarak Mandal was registered and the high school was started in 1979. Anyone who has worked in the field of education knows that it is not possible to run a private school without government aid unless it is exclusively for the rich who can pay high fees and lumpsum donations. There was another high school in a neighbouring village only about 2 kilometers from Ralegan. On this ground the state authorities refused financial grant to the Ralegan high school. The villagers ran the high school with their own money for one year and then resorted to a mass dharna outside the *Zilla Parishad*. The state education minister had to announce the grant to the school as a special case in consideration of the determination of the villagers to have their own school for better education.

The desire of the people for good educational facilities was also amply demonstrated at the time of construction of the hostel for school boys coming from neighbouring villages. The grant for the hostel building under NREP, was released like most government programs - only two months before it would lapse on account of the year ending. The village people offered *shramadaan* and worked round the clock to utilize the grant of Rs. 4 lakhs within 2 months. The completed building is now evaluated at around Rs. 16 lakhs. Now some residents of the neighbouring villages who have shifted to Bombay have also sent their children for studying in the Ralegan high school. The school has become so famous that children from far away villages also seek admission here in large numbers.

Thus, during the period 1975 to 1985, educational facilities were created ih the village in the form of a big room for a *balwadi*, a new building for the government primary school, a building for the high school run by Sant Yadav Baba Shikshan Prasarak Mandal and a hostel building. There was a large component of people's involvement in creation of these facilities in the form of *shramadaan* though, of course, government grants were taken wherever possible. Not a single rupee has been taken as donation from any funding agencies or individual philanthropists.

In the *balwadi* the average enrollment from 1976 to 1986 was of 50 children, whereas in the primary schools, from 1975 to 1978, on an average 73 children entered the first standard. Of these only 15 passed out of the 4th standard. From 1979 to 1985, on an average 55 children entered the first standard and 39 passed out of the 4th standard. In the high school, from 1979 to 1985 on an average 18 students passed the high school examination. In 1986 there were 80 children in the *balwadi*, 201 in the primary school and 353 were studying in the high school. Thirty six students including 6 girls were pursuing higher education including professional courses, after passing their School Secondary Certificate (10th standard Board) examination from Ralegan. Two girls were doing their D.Ed. (Diploma in Education) course to become teachers, four of them were in 12th standard, where like the boys they were also doing different courses in Science, Commerce, Industrial Technical Institute (ITI) and also two of them were in the Co-operatives Training Institute at Ahmednagar.

Besides these physical achievements, the major objective that the people of Ralegan wanted to accomplish with the help of education was that of making better individuals. For this purpose emphasis is laid on the physical and moral development of children by regular physical exercises, social consciousness and inculcating moral values. The programs/ methods adopted include games, music, *yogasanas*, meditation, recitation of Geeta, *Hari-Paatth* discussions with students on moral values and superstitions and involvement of students in programs like "Untouchability Eradication Fortnight", *Gram Swarajya* Camps, Adult Education Program, tree plantation and maintaining the village clean program. Special coaching is also given to children for attaining proficiency in academics.

Health Status of the People

Health of the people has long been recognised as an indicator of the quality of life. For improving the health of the people all efforts should therefore logically be directed to improving the quality of life. All health planning in our country has on the contrary, been directed towards producing more doctors, more drugs and building more hospitals. Such lopsided planning has improved the quality of life of doctors, dug companies, contractors and their middlemen, at the cost of the health of the poor people in whose name the entire health system stands today.

Ralegan has shown as to what needs to be done for better quality of life and better health of people, the latter being the consequence of the first. The most outstanding aspect of the Ralegan phenomenon has been that health of the people has improved without any special inputs into health care.

The important features of Ralegan's development with respect to quality of life have been as follows:

1. *Drinking water*: Water shortage during summer months was earlier a perennial problem in Ralegan, giving rise to gastro-intestinal ailments, diarrhoea, guinea-worm infection and many other water borne diseases. By 1986 there were eight bore wells and everyone was getting piped, potable water supply within 100 meters from their residence, without long queues and daily fights.
2. *Disposal of waste water*: Almost every house has a soak-pit outside the house to take care of the waste water coming out of the kitchen and bathroom. In the entire village one does not come across a single standing pool of waste water. Water from the piped water stand posts as well as from the public bathrooms is directed to plants and trees through cement drains.
3. *Public toilets*: Sets of toilets, urinals and bathrooms have been constructed in the village and one can see people queuing up to use them rather than defecating in the open. Public toilets have been connected to *gobar* gas plants and loose soil in the urinals is changed periodically to be used as organic compost.

4. *Gobar gas plants and smokeless chulhas*: Kitchens in Ralegan are not smoke dens any more. 28 *gobar* gas plants (many more have been added recently) and smokeless *chulhas* in 160 households have saved women from respiratory infections and sore red eyes.
5. *Nutrition*: All children in Ralegan look healthy as they get good, nutritious food at home as well as in schools. Fruits, green vegetables and milk have found a place in people's diet once their economic well-being is achieved. Fruits of trees planted on community lands are distributed in the school. The *Balwadi* children get milk as nutritional supplement from the co-operative dairy in the village. The boys staying in the hostel get nutritious meals from the community kitchen. The grain bank run by the village *Tarun Mandal* sees to it that no family in the village faces food shortage during lean periods.
6. *Mental health* : Men and women busy in their gainful vocations feel a sense of achievement when they get adequate information and guidance to improve their lot and required finance from the bank. The menfolk are no more victims of vices like alcoholism and women have no longer to drudge for water or fuel every day. The children are receiving good education in the schools. All this has made its impact on the family life which is more peaceful now. The sense of direction and a feeling of achievement is bound to have due impact on the mental and physical well-being of the people.
7. *Health care services*: The role of health care services cannot be ignored. There is a sub-centre in the village with an ANM (Anxiliary Nurse Midwife) staying there. It has responded well to the demand of basic preventive services by the people. The results are that 100% of the children are immunised, all pregnant women get antenatal care and advice including tetanus toxoid injections and Iron supplement. Eligible couple protection rate is so high that there are only 4 or 5 couples who are not coming forward for sterilisation operation even after three children. Even this high acceptance of planned family norm has come about without any intensive campaign of PHC employees coaxing people

or big industrialists offering lucrative incentives. The sub-centre also caters to curative treatment of minor ailments like minor injuries or common fevers.

Role of External Agents

There were a large number of people with whom Anna and the people of Ralegan interacted during the ten years of this study. What role these people had in the making of Anna's leadership or in making the Ralegan of today is very difficult to say. Anna deliberately kept away from the politicians. He believes that politics divides villages and thus creates obstacles in the development of villages.

Political parties or political affiliations do not play any role in the *Panchayat* elections in Ralegan. Instead, the village gets together and the *Sarpanch* as well as other members of the *Panchayat* are nominated by the villagers by consensus. Even during the Assembly or Parliament elections, the village votes by consensus after giving due consideration to the merits of the options available.

Well-known political figures like Shri Bala Saheb (R.S.) Bharde and Shri V.S. Page interacted with Anna Hazare more as Gandhians than as Congressmen. However, it appears that Anna and Ralegan Siddhi did benefit from the support provided by these two senior and respected politicians of Maharashtra. Mr. Anil Kumar Lakhina, the dynamic collector of Ahmednagar district at that time also helped a lot in getting schemes sanctioned out of turn for Ralegan. The administration's pragmatism to show results and Ralegan's capacity to successfully implement the schemes got combined with each other. The openness of Anna and the people of Ralegan in accepting ideas and assistance from different individuals and agencies have contributed to taking up of a large variety of programmes in the village. Individuals like Ashok Bedarkar, Leelatai Mulgaonkar, Navalbhau Firodia, Dr. N.H. Antia and Dr. Arole and the institutions like Rahuri Vidyapeeth and Pune University have made their contributions by interacting with Ralegan in many ways. But, in the entire development scenario, clearly, the leading role has been of the people of Ralegan, including Anna Hazare. The external agents have only played a very marginal, though useful role in the whole affair.

3

Protests by Anna Hazare

Introduction

The 2011 Indian anti-corruption movement constitutes of a series of protests for the Jan Lokpal Bill (Citizen Ombudsman Bill) that sprang up across India especially after April 5, 2011. The protesters want the Government of India to draft a strong anti-graft Lokpal bill which follows the originally drafted bill and not the changes the government plans to bring in, which will make the Lokayukta just another advisory body with no actual power in the vast Indian bureaucracy. Following continuous calls in vain to the government to work effectively towards passing the bill, a renowned civil society activist and Gandhian, Anna Hazare, went on an indefinite hunger strike unto death until his demands in support of the bill were met. Anna demanded for a joint committee of civil society members and government representatives to draft a strong anti-graft bill.

The protests led to the creation of an unprecedented movement that saw protests being organised in various cities and towns of India. Protests included fasts, candlelight vigils and rallies. The protests are especially one of their kind in India as they have no political affiliation and the protesters have been very hostile to any political party trying to grab the initiative to meet its own political goals from the activists. The protests to some extent have similarities in methodologies to Jayaprakash Narayan's Bihar Movement (commonly called the JP Movement) of 1974. There were also similarities to the methods and philosophies used in the 2011 Egyptian revolution and the Tunisian revolution, that have rocked the very foundations of governments in the Arab world.

Background

India has seen a lot of corruption in the last 60 years since independence. The economy of India was under socialist-inspired policies for an entire generation from the 1950s until the late 1980s. The economy was subject to extensive regulation, protectionism, and public ownership, leading to slow growth. There was also pervasive corruption in a system of bureaucratic controls (License Raj), which was often at the core of corruption.

The Vohra Report of 1993, submitted by the former Indian Union Home Secretary N. N. Vohra, studied the problem of the criminalisation of politics and of the nexus among criminals, politicians and bureaucrats in India. The report contained several observations made by official agencies on the criminal network which was virtually running a parallel government. It also discussed criminal gangs who enjoyed the patronage of politicians of all political parties and the protection of government functionaries. It revealed that political leaders had become the leaders of gangs. They were also connected to the military. Over the years criminals had been elected to local bodies, State Assemblies, and even the Parliament.

According to Jitendra Singh, "in the bad old days, particularly pre-1991, when the License Raj held sway, and by design, all kinds of free market mechanisms were hobbled or stymied, and corruption emerged almost as an illegitimate price mechanism, a shadowy quasi-market, such that scarce resources could still be allocated within the economy, and decisions could get made. These were largely distortions created by the politico-economic regime. While a sea change has occurred in the years following 1991, some of the distorted cultural norms that took hold during the earlier period are slowly being repaired by the sheer forces of competition. The process will be long and slow, however. It will not change overnight." One of the major problems and obstacles to development that many developing countries face is corruption by greedy, power-hungry politicians, which is endemic in certain parts of the world.

The Right to Information Act (RTI Act) that came into force in 2005 has helped civilians work effectively towards tackling corruption. The RTI Act allows all Indian citizens (except those living in Jammu and Kashmir) to request information from a "public authority" (a body of Government or "instrumentality of State") which is required to reply expeditiously or within thirty days, all for a merge sum of 10 (US$ 0.22). It has also helped activists uncover graft cases against various politicians and bureaucrats. To quell the findings made by RTI activists, there have been instances where RTI activists have been attacked and even killed in some cases.

In the period 2010-2011, India witnessed various scandals being blown apart by the media, whistle-blowers, civil society activists and government investigation agencies alike. Scams like 2G spectrum scam, Adarsh Housing Society Scam, Commonwealth Games scam and many more brought about name of various Cabinet Ministers, Chief Ministers and even members of the Armed Forces. This showed how deeply entrenched corruption has become in India. It has led to a more expansive civil society movement that wishes to fight graft with the strictest of laws and penalties. India Against Corruption is a body created by various prominent activists and the citizens of India. It has no political affiliations and only wishes to bring about drastic changes in the governance system of India so as to tackle corruption effectively.

The original idea behind the Jan Lokpal Bill is to have the independent body which would investigate cases of corruption within a year and ensure speedy trial within the next year. India Against Corruption has made it its prime objective to bring about the passing in parliament and subsequent effective enforcement of the Jan Lokpal Bill. It has also become a force organizing protests in support of the bill.

Protest Timeline

13 March 2011 (2011-03-13): A group of Delhi residents dressed in white shirts and t-shirts took a four-hour drive around the city to drum up campaign against corruption and rally support for the Jan Lokpal Bill.

28 March 2011 (2011-03-28): According to the organisers of the protests held globally on that day - "As many as 45 cities in USA, 40 cities in India and 8 other countries globally joined in an anti-corruption movement. Indians across the globe, as far as from Nagpur to New Jersey and Sydney to Seattle shouted in one voice to enact 'Jan Lokpal Bill' and ratify the UN Convention against Corruption." Many of the marchers were planning to continue the movement by joining Anna Hazare's fast in Delhi on 5 April for the same cause.

4 April 2011 (2011-04-04): Anna Hazare, the anti corruption activist leader announced his fast unto death till Jan Lokpal Bill is enacted.

5 April 2011 (2011-04-05)

- Anna Hazare, initiated his fast unto death at Jantar Mantar in Delhi
- Around 6,000 Mumbai residents joined Anna Hazare for a one-day fast to support the demand for implementation of the Jan Lokpal Bill.
- In Pune over 6,000 residents joined the campaign.
- The Freedom Park in Banglore was the cynosure of all eyes on Thursday as Bangaloreans from all walks of life thronged the place to support Anna Hazare.

7 April 2011 (2011-04-07)

- 2 rounds of talks with the government failed.
- Anna Hazare continued on with his fast.
- Narendra Modi, the chief Minister of Gujarat lashes out at Manmohan Singh for resisting the passage of the Jan Lokpal Bill
- Sonia Gandhi, the president of the Indian National Congress party and the head of the National Advisory Council appealed to Anna Hazare to end his indefinite fast.

8 April 2011 (2011-04-08)

- Protests spreaded to Mumbai, Kolkata, Hyderabad, Bangalore, Chennai, Patna, Bhopal, Ahmedabad, Ranchi, Pune, Nashik and Kochi.

- Protests were organised at Jammu University in Jammu, Thiruvananthapuram, Guwahati and Jaipur too.
- The government continued to squabble with the activists stating that the bill drafting committee will be headed by a government appointed minister and not a civil society member as the protesters demanded to avoid allowing the government to make the bill less powerful.
- The Prime Minister Dr. Manmohan Singh met with the President of India to outline to her how the government was going ahead with the demands of the population.
- 15 supporters of Anna Hazare on fast were hospitalized.
- Bollywood came out completely in support of the protests - with famed actors, musicians and directors speaking in support of the movement and Anna Hazare. Director Farah Khan, actor Anupam Kher, music director Vishal Dadlani, poet-filmmaker Pritish Nandy and actor Tom Alter all visited Jantar Mantar. Meanwhile famed Indian actors Aamir Khan, Hrithik Roshan and Amitabh Bachchan all stated their support for the movement via social networking websites or the media. Oscar winning Indian composer A. R. Rahman also declared his support for the anti-graft movement. Kareena Kapoor, Shabana Azmi,Shekhar Kapur, Sushmita Sen, Bipasha Basu, Shahid Kapoor, Riteish Deshmukh, Vivek Oberoi, Neha Dhupia,Jackky Bhagnani, Shirish Kunder, Kailash Kher, Punit Malhotra all tweeted their support for Anna Hazare further feulling the masses to join the movement.
- Famed Qatari artist M. F. Hussain showed his support by drawing a cartoon of Anna Hazare.
- Indian students at Cambridge University, the former alma-mater of the Indian prime minister also addressed their support for the movement.
- Many prominent people from the government agencies as well as from various corporate houses came out in support of the movement. Some of them were - Delhi Metro chief E. Sreedharan (also called the Metro Man of India), Punj Lloyd chairman Atul Punj, Maruti Suzuki chairman RC Bhargava, Hero group's Sunil Munjal, Tata Steel vice-chairman B

Muthuraman, Bajaj Auto Chairman Rahul Bajaj, Godrej Group head Adi Godrej, Biocon Chairman and Managing Director Kiran Mazumdar-Shaw and Kotak Mahindra Bank vice-chairman & managing director Uday Kotak. They all declared their support for Anna Hazare and the movement.

- ASSOCHAM President Dilip Modi and FICCI Director General Rajiv Kumar, both came out in support of the movement too.
- The Government of India accepted the compromise formula that there be a politician chairman and an activist, non-politician Co-Chairman. It was reported that Pranab Mukherjee will be the Chairman of the draft committee while Shanti Bhushan will be the co-chairman. Shanti Bhushan was one of the original drafters of the Lokpal Bill along with Anna Hazare, Justice N. Santosh Hegde, advocate Prashant Bhushan, and RTI activist Arvind Kejriwal.

9 April 2011 (2011-04-09)

- After accepting all the demands of Anna Hazare, the Government of India issued a Official Gazette saying that the draft of lokpal would be made and presented in the coming monsoon session of Lok Sabha.
- Victory celebrations were held all over India from Jantar Mantar - the center of the protests to Hyderabad, Jammu, Mumbai, Nagpur, Chennai, Kolkatta, Allahabad and even Anna Hazare's village.
- Bollywood lauded the victory of Anna Hazare, once again echoing their support for the movement and the support of the Indian citizenry.
- Anti-Corruption protestors at India Gate booed and drove away controversial journalist Barkha Dutt.
- Protesters and leaders of the movement alike stated that the path to attaining complete passing of the bill is still a difficult one, and the movement has to see more harsher days ahead.
- The movement has become a symbol of civil society's power in India. After being widely televised by the Indian media, and widely supported by almost every Indian citizen (as the issue of corruption has been an issue every Indian holds very negative views about), the movement has attained a

certain level of credibility in the eyes of the Indian masses. Its uniqueness in the fact that it was completely apolitical; was a movement solely of the people; did not wish to put in disarray the country as in the case of total shutdowns organised by political parties (Commonly called a Bandh) ; and was able to bend the government - is something new for India. Many commentators have called the movement the 'wake-up' call for India. Meanwhile social networking chatter has been filled with fears that Indians will once again go back to 'sleep' with time.

Drafting Committee of the Bill

The 10 member Drafting Committee of the Jan Lokpal Bill will have an equal representation of both politicians and civil society members. On 8 April 2011, the Ministry of Law and Justice issued an official notification, The Gazette of India, regarding the Joint Drafting Committee of the bill. A copy of the notification can be found here.

Chairman

The Government of India accepted that there be a politician Chairman and an activist, non-politician Co-Chairman. It is reported that Pranab Mukherjee, from the political arena, and Shanti Bhushan, from the civil society, will be the Chairmen of the Drafting Committee.

Government Representation

Five Cabinet ministers will be a part of the Drafting Committee. They are:

1. Pranab Mukherjee, Finance Minister of India, *Co-Chairman*
2. P. Chidambaram, Minister of Home Affairs, *Panel Member*
3. Veerappa Moily, Minister of Law and Justice, *Panel Member*
4. Kapil Sibal, Minister for Communications and Information Technology, *Panel Member*
5. Salman Khursid, Minister of Water Resources, *Panel Member*

Civil Society Representation

Five leading socialists will be a part of the Drafting Committee. They are:

1. Shanti Bhushan, Former Minister of Law and Justice, *Co-Chairman*
2. Anna Hazare, Social Activist, *Panel Member*
3. Prashant Bhushan, Lawyer, *Panel Member*
4. N. Santosh Hegde, Lokayukta (Karnataka), *Panel Member*
5. Arvind Kejriwal, RTI activist, *Panel Member*

Allegations against panel members: Adding a new chapter in Lokpal Bill issue, the candidature of Shanti Bhushan, veteran lawyer, former union law minister and co-chairman of the new committee formed as a result of Anna Hazare's recent hunger strike to draft a law on corruption, has come under scanner after a new CD controversy. Shanti Bhushan said that "it certainly appears to be a motivated, mallicious campaign to derail the draft of the Lokpal bill.". Some pro-corruption supporters or those who would benefit from the status quo are drumming up support against this anti corruption movement by using the usual old tactics of attempting to cast doubt on Anna Hazare, the committee members, the who movement and how it was handled in the media and the press etc.

First Lokpal Bill draft meeting: First Lokpal Bill draft meeting was held on 16 April 2011, Eight days after Gandhian Anna Hazare called off his fast demanding a stronger Lokpal law. The government has agreed to audio-recording of all meetings of the Lokpal Bill panel and to holding public consultations before a final draft of the anti-graft law is prepared. Next meeting will be held on 2 May 2011. Anna Hazare insisted to telecast the live proceedings video, but government denied stating certain "drawbacks" of doing so and so the first meeting was held recording the audio for future references.

Use of Social Networks

Within a day of the beginning of the agitation, more than 30,000 people pledged their support to the Lokpal Bill. Organisers of the India Against Corruption said 30,000 people from Maharashtra expressed their support on their website. With an active Facebook page comprising of over 60,000 fans and a Twitter profile with more than 3300 followers, the "India Against Corruption" movement has already been a big success. The website has 20,000 members in Mumbai alone. Within a few days the Facebook page for India Against Corruption had more than 150,000 likes. There was heightened political activity on social networking websites like Twitter and Facebook. Various support group pages and events were created on the websites to show support and rally the masses.

Nonpartisan Nature

Hazare and the protesters have tried to keep the protests non-political. No politicians were welcome at the site of the fast. Former Haryana Chief Minister Om Prakash Chautala, former Madhya Pradesh Chief Minister Uma Bharti and pro Sonia Gandhi journalist Barkha Dutt were forced by civilians to leave, after the protesters objected against their presence which they believed was harming the integrity of their movement.

Government Response

Hazare's protest has led to the resignation of Agriculture Minister Sharad Pawar from the Group of Ministers on corruption after Anna took potshots at him. On 8 April, the government started seriously considering the demands of the protesters. The government has stated that it will table the bill in the parliament in the upcoming Monsoon session. On 9 April, the government finally agreed to have a 50:50 distribution of the Government appointed officials and the members of the civil society.

Political Response

Bhartiya Janata Party: Bhartiya Janata Party supported Anna Hazare. Senior Bharatiya Janata Party (BJP) leader Arun Jaitley urged the Congress-led UPA Government to take veteran social activist Anna's indefinite fast very seriously.

Senior BJP leader, L.K. Advani suggested that a meeting of political parties should be convened to discuss this issue "particularly in the context of black money and curbing money-power in elections".

BJP leader and Chief Minister of Gujarat Narendra Modi posted on his Facebook account that he was diligently praying for Anna Hazare's health. He also published an open letter to Anna Hazare thanking him for the latter's support for the development work in Gujarat (being spearheaded by Narendra Modi himself as the chief minister of the state). Narendra Modi also cautioned Anna Hazare of possible vilification by a certain 'powerful-group' that wishes to defame Narendra Modi and Gujarat. He reiterated his support for the Jan Lokpal Bill, stating that he was also just another common man.

Communist Party of India (Marxist): The Communist Party of India (Marxist) came out in support of Anna Hazare. Prakash Karat pledged support to Hazare over the Jan Lokpal Bill.

Indian Black Money in Swiss Banks

Swami Ramdev has also publicly raised the issue of Indian money stashed away illegally in Swiss bank which is estimated to be between 1-1.5 trillion USD. He says that the government must take concrete action and bring back the money as it belongs to the people of India and has been taken out of the country illegally. The bill is a first step towards anti-corruption measures and will not be complete without addressing certain major reformations like bringing back black money. He wanted the government to make it mandatory for those who have deposited money in foreign banks to declare them and also to close the Mauritius route, which is a haven for tax evaders.

Amount of Money

Though the exact amount of money is not known. There are reports in media that 500 Lakh crores of black money of Indian origin is in foreign banks. India tops the list for black money in the entire world with almost US$1456 billion in Swiss banks (USD 1.4 trillion approximately) in the form of black money. According to the data provided by the Swiss Banking Association Report (2006), India has more black money than the rest of the world combined. Indian Swiss bank account assets are worth 13 times the country's national debt. Indian black money is sometimes physically transferred abroad.

The CEO of a Mumbai-based equity firm recently told journalists that the money is flown abroad in "special flights" out of Mumbai and Delhi airports to Zurich. Indeed Indians would be the largest depositors of illegal money in Swiss banks, according to sources in the banking industry. The estimated average amount stashed away annually from India during 2002–2006 is $27.3 billion US dollars.

Havens for Black Money

Switzerland: Switzerland is the top destination for illegal funds because of its strict secrecy laws. Also, Swiss banks sell additional masks to hide the identity of their rich clients, like trusts in the Cayman islands, shell companies in Panama, or foundations in Liechtenstein, all run by nominees.

Mauritius Route

Other Foreign Banks

Banks in other countries are also reported to have accounts where Indian black money have been deposited as per reports.

Supreme court's displeasure: The Supreme Court have chided the government for restricting names of those with black money stashed abroad in Liechtenstein Bank in Germany.

Government Response: The government is ready to share information with the Supreme Court but is not making it public. It says that it is in the process of getting more details of foreign accounts of Indians from other countries under the DTAA regime.

Satyagraha against Corruption (SAC)

Swami Ramdev declared that a people's movement to liberate the country from rampant corruption and build a strong spiritual 'Bharat' would be launched by him in June. The movement which is second phase of Bharath Swabhiman Yatra is named 'Satyagraha against Corruption'. He declared one of the main objectives of the movement was to bring about an end to corruption and bring back black money stashed away in various financial institutions in the country and abroad.

❑❑❑

4

Right to Information Movement

Introduction

The President of India appoints Civil Servants in Indian Administrative Services (IAS), Indian Police Services (IPS) and Indian Forest Services (IFS). The People's Representatives and the Civil Servants are ultimately the public servants. They have to serve the citizens. But, the picture is altogether different today. The People's Representatives and the Civil Servants have become masters of the country and made the citizens poor servants. In the Maharashtra State, a campaign was started demanding for the Right to Information. As Peoples Representatives and Civil Servants are public servants and the citizens of Maharashtra are owners of the public money, the citizens have the right to ask the public servants how and in what manner they spend the public money. He pressed for legislating an Act for Right to Information. The first campaign was organized at the Azad Maidan, Mumbai, in 1997. The State Government was giving only promises, but it failed to crystallize it in many sessions of the Vidhan Sabha. He had to make agitations, dharnas, morchas, maun and fasts many times.

State-wide tours were held for awareness generation among people. Public addresses were organized in many towns and programmes were arranged specially for college students. Posters, banners and folders were printed and distributed in thousands. All this resulted in the awakening of the citizens and making them aware of their fundamental Right to Information.

The Government made many promises, but it failed to keep one. Any government never wants to decentralize its power and hand over power to people. Many politicians think that decentralization of power will lessen their importance, status and respect. So the Government was reluctant to make legislation for Right to Information.

Finally, with zeal of 'do-or-die', Mr. Hazare went on fast-unto-death on August 9, 2003 at Azad Maidan, Mumbai. He decided that unless the Act is passed by the Government, he will not end his fast; rather he will sacrifice his life for peoples rights.

The Government of Maharashtra felt that his resolution is firm and He would not step back from his decision of 'do-or-die'. On the 12th day of his fast, the Government of Maharashtra got the Bill signed by the President of India and enacted the law of 'Right to Information' in Maharashtra. The Act on 'Right to Information' is a revolutionary step towards strengthening democracy.

This Act has enabled the common man to seek information. Till to-date, the people have to obey the laws; whereas the government machinery controlled everything. But by the advent of this Act, the Government Agencies have to obey the law and the people have got controlling power.

This Act should have come into force on 26th February 1950 itself; the day India celebrated its first Republic Day. This would have brought transparency and accountability in every transaction of the government and would have checked corruption to a great extent. The erstwhile British rulers had prohibited people from getting any information by creating the Official Secrets Act. The following Indian governments maintained status quo by not amending the Act as it provided them space for corruption. The British Act of Official Secrets was in force for almost 58 years after British left India. This Act gave the weapon in the hands of corrupt politicians and officers to exploit the common man.

Under the guise of the Official secrets Act, information was denied to people. So he started the movement for Right to Information. In freedom, every citizen has fundamental right to know how the public money is spent. The question to the Government was "Why do you deny information which is not confidential" under the guise of Official Secrets Act? Finally, the government had to make the Right to Information Act.

Due to this Act, transparency has come in the administration. Now a common man can get information by just paying a nominal charge of Rs. 10 or 20. This has paved the way to good governance and healthy democracy.

If this Act reaches every village and every household, it has potential to check corruption to an extent of 80 - 85%. Due to corruption, only 10 percent could reach the real beneficiaries of the poverty alleviation programmes earlier. Rest of the money percolated to the purses of corrupt officers and politicians. Now, due to the Act of Right to Information, the poor villagers will get their due share in the development process. The quality of project works has started to improve after the Act.

THE RIGHT TO INFORMATION ACT, 2005
No. 22 of 2005 [15th June, 2005]

An Act to provide for setting out the practical regime of right to information for citizens to secure access to information under the control of public authorities, in order to promote transparency and accountability in the working of every public authority, the constitution of a Central Information Commission and State Information Commissions and for matters connected therewith or incidental thereto.

Whereas the Constitution of India has established democratic Republic; And whereas democracy requires an informed citizenry and transparency of information which are vital to its functioning and also to contain corruption and to hold Governments and their instrumentalities accountable to the governed; And whereas revelation of information in actual practice is likely to conflict with other public interests including efficient operations of the Governments, optimum use of limited fiscal resources and the preservation of confidentiality of sensitive information; And whereas it is necessary to harmonise these conflicting interests while preserving the paramountcy of the democratic ideal; Now, therefore, it is expedient to provide for furnishing certain information to citizens who desire to have it. Be it enacted by Parliament in the Fifty-sixth Year of the Republic of India as follows: –

CHAPTER - I : PRELIMINARY

1 (1) This Act may be called the Right to Information Act, 2005.

(2) It extends to the whole of India except the State of Jammu and Kashmir.

(3) The provisions of sub-section (*1*) of section 4, sub-sections (*1*) and (*2*) of section 5, sections 12, 13, 15,16, 24 , 27 and 28 shall come into force at once, and the remaining provisions of this Act shall come into force on the one hundred and twentieth day of its enactment.

2. In this Act, unless the context otherwise requires, –

(a) "appropriate Government" means in relation to a public authority which is established, constituted, owned, controlled or substantially financed by funds provided directly or indirectly –

(i) by the Central Government or the Union territory administration, the Central Government;

(ii) by the State Government, the State Government;

(b) "Central Information Commission" means the Central Information Commission constituted under sub-section (*1*) of section 12;

(c) "Central Public Information Officer" means the Central Public Information Officer designated under sub-section (*1*) and includes a Central Assistant Public Information Officer designated as such under sub-section (*2*) of section 5;

(d) "Chief Information Commissioner" and "Information Commissioner" mean the Chief Information Commissioner and Information Commissioner appointed under sub-section (*3*) of section 12;

(e) "competent authority" means –

(i) the Speaker in the case of the House of the People or the Legislative Assembly of a State or a Union territory having such Assembly and the Chairman in the case of the Council of States or Legislative Council of a State;

(ii) the Chief Justice of India in the case of the Supreme Court;

(iii) the Chief Justice of the High Court in the case of a High Court;

(iv) the President or the Governor, as the case may be, in the case of other authorities established or constituted by or under the Constitution;

(v) the administrator appointed under article 239 of the Constitution;

(f) "information" means any material in any form, including records, documents, memos, e-mails, opinions, advices, press releases, circulars, orders, logbooks, contracts, reports, papers, samples, models, data material held in any electronic form and information relating to any private body which can be accessed by a public authority under any other law for the time being in force;

(g) "prescribed" means prescribed by rules made under this Act by the appropriate Government or the competent authority, as the case may be;

(h) "public authority" means any authority or body or institution of self- government established or constituted –

(a) by or under the Constitution;

(b) by any other law made by Parliament;

(c) by any other law made by State Legislature;

(d) by notification issued or order made by the appropriate Government, and includes any –

(i) body owned, controlled or substantially financed;

(ii) non-Government organization substantially financed, directly or indirectly by funds provided by the appropriate Government;

(i) "record" includes –

(a) any document, manuscript and file;

(b) any microfilm, microfiche and facsimile copy of a document;

(c) any reproduction of image or images embodied in such microfilm (whether enlarged or not); and

(d) any other material produced by a computer or any other device;

(j) "right to information" means the right to information accessible under this Act which is held by or under the control of any public authority and includes the right to –

(i) inspection of work, documents, records;

(ii) taking notes, extracts or certified copies of documents or records;

(iii) taking certified samples of material;

(iv) obtaining information in the form of diskettes, floppies, tapes, video cassettes or in any other electronic mode or through printouts where such information is stored in a computer or in any other device;

(k) "State Information Commission" means the State Information Commission constituted under sub-section (*1*) of section 15;

(l) "State Chief Information Commissioner" and "State Information Commissioner" mean the State Chief Information Commissioner and the State Information Commissioner appointed under sub-section (*3*) of section 15;

(m) "State Public Information Officer" means the State Public Information Officer designated under sub-section (*1*) and includes a State Assistant Public

Information Officer designated as such under sub-section (2) of section 5;

(n) "third party" means a person other than the citizen making a request for information and includes a public authority.

CHAPTER - II : RIGHT TO INFORMATION AND OBLIGATIONS OF PUBLIC AUTHORITIES

3. Subject to the provisions of this Act, all citizens shall have the right to information.

4.(1) Every public authority shall—

(a) maintain all its records duly catalogued and indexed in a manner and the form which facilitates the right to information under this Act and ensure that all records that are appropriate to be computerised are, within a reasonable time and subject to availability of resources, computerised and connected through a network all over the country on different systems so that access to such records is facilitated;

(b) publish within one hundred and twenty days from the enactment of this Act,—

(i) the particulars of its organisation, functions and duties;

(ii) the powers and duties of its officers and employees;

(iii) the procedure followed in the decision making process, including channels of supervision and accountability;

(iv) the norms set by it for the discharge of its functions;

(v) the rules, regulations, instructions, manuals and records, held by it or under its control or used by its employees for discharging its functions;

(vi) a statement of the categories of documents that are held by it or under its control;

(vii) the particulars of any arrangement that exists for consultation with, or representation by, the members of the public in relation to the formulation of its policy or implementation thereof;

(viii) a statement of the boards, councils, committees and other bodies consisting of two or more persons constituted as its part or for the purpose of its advice, and as to whether meetings of those boards, councils, committees and other bodies are open to the public, or the minutes of such meetings are accessible for public;

(ix) a directory of its officers and employees;

(x) the monthly remuneration received by each of its officers and employees, including the system of compensation as provided in its regulations;

(xi) the budget allocated to each of its agency, indicating the particulars of all plans, proposed expenditures and reports on disbursements made;

(xii) the manner of execution of subsidy programmes, including the amounts allocated and the details of beneficiaries of such programmes;

(xiii) particulars of recipients of concessions, permits or authorisations granted by it;

(xiv) details in respect of the information, available to or held by it, reduced in an electronic form;

(xv) the particulars of facilities available to citizens for obtaining information, including the working hours of a library or reading room, if maintained for public use;

(xvi) the names, designations and other particulars of the Public Information Officers;

(xvii) such other information as may be prescribed and thereafter update these publications every year;

(c) publish all relevant facts while formulating important policies or announcing the decisions which affect public;

(d) provide reasons for its administrative or quasi-judicial decisions to affected persons.

(2) It shall be a constant endeavour of every public authority to take steps in accordance with the requirements of clause (b) of sub-section (1) to provide as much information suo motu to the public at regular intervals through various means of communications, including internet, so that the public have minimum resort to the use of this Act to obtain information.

(3) For the purposes of sub-section (1), every information shall be disseminated widely and in such form and manner which is easily accessible to the public.

(4) All materials shall be disseminated taking into consideration the cost effectiveness, local language and the most effective method of communication in that local area and the information should be easily accessible, to the extent possible in electronic format with the Central Public Information Officer or State Public Information Officer, as the case may be, available free or at such cost of the medium or the print cost price as may be prescribed.

Explanation. For the purposes of sub-sections (3) and (4), "disseminated" means making known or communicated the information to the public through notice boards, newspapers, public announcements, media broadcasts, the internet or any other means, including inspection of offices of any public authority.

5. (1) Every public authority shall, within one hundred days of the enactment of this Act, designate as many officers as the Central Public Information Officers or State Public Information Officers, as the case may be, in all administrative units or offices under it as may be necessary to provide information to persons requesting for the information under this Act.

(2) Without prejudice to the provisions of sub-section (1), every public authority shall designate an officer, within one hundred days of the enactment of this Act, at each sub-divisional level or other sub-district level as a Central Assistant Public Information Officer or a State Assistant Public Information Officer, as the case may be, to receive the

applications for information or appeals under this Act for forwarding the same forthwith to the Central Public Information Officer or the State Public Information Officer or senior officer specified under sub-section (1) of section 19 or the Central Information Commission or the State Information Commission, as the case may be: Provided that where an application for information or appeal is given to a Central Assistant Public Information Officer or a State Assistant Public Information Officer, as the case may be, a period of five days shall be added in computing the period for response specified under sub-section (1) of section 7.

(3) Every Central Public Information Officer or State Public Information Officer, as the case may be, shall deal with requests from persons seeking information and render reasonable assistance to the persons seeking such information.

(4) The Central Public Information Officer or State Public Information Officer, as the case may be, may seek the assistance of any other officer as he or she considers it necessary for the proper discharge of his or her duties.

(5) Any officer, whose assistance has been sought under sub-section (4), shall render all assistance to the Central Public Information Officer or State Public Information Officer, as the case may be, seeking his or her assistance and for the purposes of any contravention of the provisions of this Act, such other officer shall be treated as a Central Public Information Officer or State Public Information Officer, as the case may be.

6. (1) A person, who desires to obtain any information under this Act, shall make a request in writing or through electronic means in English or Hindi or in the official language of the area in which the application is being made, accompanying such fee as may be prescribed, to—

(a) the Central Public Information Officer or State Public Information Officer, as the case may be, of the concerned public authority;

(b) the Central Assistant Public Information Officer or State Assistant Public Information Officer, as the case may be, specifying the particulars of the information sought by him or her:Provided that where such request cannot be made in writing, the Central Public Information Officer or State Public Information Officer, as the case may be, shall render all reasonable assistance to the person making the request orally to reduce the same in writing.

(2) An applicant making request for information shall not be required to give any reason for requesting the information or any other personal details except those that may be necessary for contacting him.

(3) Where an application is made to a public authority requesting for an information,—

(i) which is held by another public authority; or

(ii) the subject matter of which is more closely connected with the functions of another public authority,the public authority, to which such application is made, shall transfer the application or such part of it as may be appropriate to that other public authority and inform the applicant immediately about such transfer: *Provided that the transfer of an application pursuant to this sub-section shall be made as soon as practicable but in no case later than five days from the date of receipt of the application.*

7. (1) Subject to the proviso to sub-section (2) of section 5 or the proviso to sub-section (3) of section 6, the Central Public Information Officer or State Public Information Officer, as the case may be, on receipt of a request under section 6 shall, as expeditiously as possible, and in any case within thirty days of the receipt of the request, either provide the information on payment of such fee as may be prescribed or reject the request for any of the reasons specified in sections 8 and 9: Provided that where the information sought for concerns the life or liberty of a person, the same shall be provided within forty-eight hours of the receipt of the request.

(2) If the Central Public Information Officer or State Public Information Officer, as the case may be, fails to give decision

on the request for information within the period specified under sub-section (1), the Central Public Information Officer or State Public Information Officer, as the case may be, shall be deemed to have refused the request.

(3) Where a decision is taken to provide the information on payment of any further fee representing the cost of providing the information, the Central Public Information Officer or State Public Information Officer, as the case may be, shall send an intimation to the person making the request, giving—

   (a) the details of further fees representing the cost of providing the information as determined by him, together with the calculations made to arrive at the amount in accordance with fee prescribed under sub-section (1), requesting him to deposit that fees, and the period intervening between the dispatch of the said intimation and payment of fees shall be excluded for the purpose of calculating the period of thirty days referred to in that sub-section;

   (b) information concerning his or her right with respect to review the decision as to the amount of fees charged or the form of access provided, including the particulars of the appellate authority, time limit, process and any other forms.

(4) Where access to the record or a part thereof is required to be provided under this Act and the person to whom access is to be provided is sensorial disabled, the Central Public Information Officer or State Public Information Officer, as the case may be, shall provide assistance to enable access to the information, including providing such assistance as may be appropriate for the inspection.

(5) Where access to information is to be provided in the printed or in any electronic format, the applicant shall, subject to the provisions of sub-section (6), pay such fee as may be prescribed: Provided that the fee prescribed under sub-section (1) of section 6 and sub-sections (1) and (5) of section 7 shall be reasonable and no such fee shall be charged from

the persons who are of below poverty line as may be determined by the appropriate Government.

(6) Notwithstanding anything contained in sub-section (5), the person making request for the information shall be provided the information free of charge where a public authority fails to comply with the time limits specified in sub-section (1).

(7) Before taking any decision under sub-section (1), the Central Public Information Officer or State Public Information Officer, as the case may be, shall take into consideration the representation made by a third party under section 11.

(8) Where a request has been rejected under sub-section (1), the Central Public Information Officer or State Public Information Officer, as the case may be, shall communicate to the person making the request, —

(i) the reasons for such rejection;

(ii) the period within which an appeal against such rejection may be preferred; and

(iii) the particulars of the appellate authority.

(9) An information shall ordinarily be provided in the form in which it is sought unless it would disproportionately divert the resources of the public authority or would be detrimental to the safety or preservation of the record in question.

8. (1) Notwithstanding anything contained in this Act, there shall be no obligation to give any citizen, —

(a) information, disclosure of which would prejudicially affect the sovereignty and integrity of India, the security, strategic, scientific or economic interests of the State, relation with foreign State or lead to incitement of an offence;

(b) information which has been expressly forbidden to be published by any court of law or tribunal or the disclosure of which may constitute contempt of court;

(c) information, the disclosure of which would cause a breach of privilege of Parliament or the State Legislature;

(d) information including commercial confidence, trade secrets or intellectual property, the disclosure of which would harm the competitive position of a third party, unless the competent authority is satisfied that larger public interest warrants the disclosure of such information;

(e) information available to a person in his fiduciary relationship, unless the competent authority is satisfied that the larger public interest warrants the disclosure of such information;

(f) information received in confidence from foreign Government;

(g) information, the disclosure of which would endanger the life or physical safety of any person or identify the source of information or assistance given in confidence for law enforcement or security purposes;

(h) information which would impede the process of investigation or apprehension or prosecution of offenders;

(i) cabinet papers including records of deliberations of the Council of Ministers, Secretaries and other officers:

Provided that the decisions of Council of Ministers, the reasons thereof, and the material on the basis of which the decisions were taken shall be made public after the decision has been taken, and the matter is complete, or over:

Provided further that those matters which come under the exemptions specified in this section shall not be disclosed;

(j) information which relates to personal information the disclosure of which has no relationship to any public activity or interest, or which would cause unwarranted invasion of the privacy of the individual unless the Central Public Information Officer or the State Public Information Officer or the appellate authority, as the case may be, is satisfied that the larger public interest justifies the disclosure of such information:

Provided that the information which cannot be denied to the Parliament or a State Legislature shall not be denied to any person.

(2) Notwithstanding anything in the Official Secrets Act, 1923 nor any of the exemptions permissible in accordance with sub-section (1), a public authority may allow access to information, if public interest in disclosure outweighs the harm to the protected interests.

(3) Subject to the provisions of clauses (a), (c) and (i) of sub-section (1), any information relating to any occurrence, event or matter which has taken place, occurred or happened twenty years before the date on which any request is made under secton 6 shall be provided to any person making a request under that section:

Provided that where any question arises as to the date from which the said period of twenty years has to be computed, the decision of the Central Government shall be final, subject to the usual appeals provided for in this Act.

9. Without prejudice to the provisions of section 8, a Central Public Information Officer or a State Public Information Officer, as the case may be, may reject a request for information where such a request for providing access would involve an infringement of copyright subsisting in a person other than the State.

10. (1) Where a request for access to information is rejected on the ground that it is in relation to information which is exempt from disclosure, then, notwithstanding anything contained in this Act, access may be provided to that part of the record which does not contain any information which is exempt from disclosure under this Act and which can reasonably be severed from any part that contains exempt information.

(2) Where access is granted to a part of the record under sub-section (1), the Central Public Information Officer or State Public Information Officer, as the case may be, shall give a notice to the applicant, informing—

(a) that only part of the record requested, after severance of the record containing information which is exempt from disclosure, is being provided;

(b) the reasons for the decision, including any findings on any material question of fact, referring to the material on which those findings were based;

(c) the name and designation of the person giving the decision;

(d) the details of the fees calculated by him or her and the amount of fee which the applicant is required to deposit; and

(e) his or her rights with respect to review of the decision regarding non-disclosure of part of the information, the amount of fee charged or the form of access provided, including the particulars of the senior officer specified under sub-section (1) of section 19 or the Central Information Commission or the State Information Commission, as the case may be, time limit, process and any other form of access.

11. (1) Where a Central Public Information Officer or a State Public Information Officer, as the case may be, intends to disclose any information or record, or part thereof on a request made under this Act, which relates to or has been supplied by a third party and has been treated as confidential by that third party, the Central Public Information Officer or State Public Information Officer, as the case may be, shall, within five days from the receipt of the request, give a written notice to such third party of the request and of the fact that the Central Public Information Officer or State Public Information Officer, as the case may be, intends to disclose the information or record, or part thereof, and invite the third party to make a submission in writing or orally, regarding whether the information should be disclosed, and such submission of the third party shall be kept in view while taking a decision about disclosure of information: Provided that except in the case of trade or commercial secrets protected by law, disclosure may be allowed if the

public interest in disclosure outweighs in importance any possible harm or injury to the interests of such third party.

(2) Where a notice is served by the Central Public Information Officer or State Public Information Officer, as the case may be, under sub-section (1) to a third party in respect of any information or record or part thereof, the third party shall, within ten days from the date of receipt of such notice, be given the opportunity to make representation against the proposed disclosure.

(3) Notwithstanding anything contained in section 7, the Central Public Information Officer or State Public Information Officer, as the case may be, shall, within forty days after receipt of the request under section 6, if the third party has been given an opportunity to make representation under sub-section (2), make a decision as to whether or not to disclose the information or record or part thereof and give in writing the notice of his decision to the third party.

(4) A notice given under sub-section (3) shall include a statement that the third party to whom the notice is given is entitled to prefer an appeal under section 19 against the decision.

CHAPTER - III : THE CENTRAL INFORMATION COMMISSION

12. (1) The Central Government shall, by notification in the Official Gazette, constitute a body to be known as the Central Information Commission to exercise the powers conferred on, and to perform the functions assigned to, it under this Act.

(2) The Central Information Commission shall consist of—

(a) the Chief Information Commissioner; and

(b) such number of Central Information Commissioners, not exceeding ten, as may be deemed necessary.

(3) The Chief Information Commissioner and Information Commissioners shall be appointed by the President on the recommendation of a committee consisting of—

(i) the Prime Minister, who shall be the Chairperson of the committee;

(ii) the Leader of Opposition in the Lok Sabha; and

(iii) a Union Cabinet Minister to be nominated by the Prime Minister.

Explanation. For the purposes of removal of doubts, it is hereby declared that where the Leader of Opposition in the House of the People has not been recognised as such, the Leader of the single largest group in opposition of the Government in the House of the People shall be deemed to be the Leader of Opposition.

(4) The general superintendence, direction and management of the affairs of the Central Information Commission shall vest in the Chief Information Commissioner who shall be assisted by the Information Commissioners and may exercise all such powers and do all such acts and things which may be exercised or done by the Central Information Commission autonomously without being subjected to directions by any other authority under this Act.

(5) The Chief Information Commissioner and Information Commissioners shall be persons of eminence in public life with wide knowledge and experience in law, science and technology, social service, management, journalism, mass media or administration and governance.

(6) The Chief Information Commissioner or an Information Commissioner shall not be a Member of Parliament or Member of the Legislature of any State or Union territory, as the case may be, or hold any other office of profit or connected with any political party or carrying on any business or pursuing any profession.

(7) The headquarters of the Central Information Commission shall be at Delhi and the Central Information Commission may, with the previous approval of the Central Government, establish offices at other places in India.

13. (1) The Chief Information Commissioner shall hold office for a term of five years from the date on which he enters upon his office and shall not be eligible for reappointment:

Provided that no Chief Information Commissioner shall hold office as such after he has attained the age of sixty-five years.

(2) Every Information Commissioner shall hold office for a term of five years from the date on which he enters upon his office or till he attains the age of sixty-five years, whichever is earlier, and shall not be eligible for reappointment as such Information Commissioner:

Provided that every Information Commissioner shall, on vacating his office under this sub-section be eligible for appointment as the Chief Information Commissioner in the manner specified in sub-section (3) of section 12:

Provided further that where the Information Commissioner is appointed as the Chief Information Commissioner, his term of office shall not be more than five years in aggregate as the Information Commissioner and the Chief Information Commissioner.

(3) The Chief Information Commissioner or an Information Commissioner shall before he enters upon his office make and subscribe before the President or some other person appointed by him in that behalf, an oath or affirmation according to the form set out for the purpose in the First Schedule.

(4) The Chief Information Commissioner or an Information Commissioner may, at any time, by writing under his hand addressed to the President, resign from his office:

Provided that the Chief Information Commissioner or an Information Commissioner may be removed in the manner specified under section 14.

(5) The salaries and allowances payable to and other terms and conditions of service of –

(a) the Chief Information Commissioner shall be the same as that of the Chief Election Commissioner;

(b) an Information Commissioner shall be the same as that of an Election Commissioner:

Provided that if the Chief Information Commissioner or an Information Commissioner, at the time of his appointment is, in receipt of a pension, other than a disability or wound pension, in respect of any previous service under the Government of India or under the Government of a State, his salary in respect of the service as the Chief Information Commissioner or an Information Commissioner shall be reduced by the amount of that pension including any portion of pension which was commuted and pension equivalent of other forms of retirement benefits excluding pension equivalent of retirement gratuity:

Provided further that if the Chief Information Commissioner or an Information Commissioner if, at the time of his appointment is, in receipt of retirement benefits in respect of any previous service rendered in a Corporation established by or under any Central Act or State Act or a Government company owned or controlled by the Central Government or the State Government, his salary in respect of the service as the Chief Information Commissioner or an Information Commissioner shall be reduced by the amount of pension equivalent to the retirement benefits:

Provided also that the salaries, allowances and other conditions of service of the Chief Information Commissioner and the Information Commissioners shall not be varied to their disadvantage after their appointment.

(6) The Central Government shall provide the Chief Information Commissioner and the Information Commissioners with such officers and employees as may be necessary for the efficient performance of their functions under this Act, and the salaries and allowances payable to and the terms and conditions of service of the officers and other employees appointed for the purpose of this Act shall be such as may be prescribed.

14. (1) Subject to the provisions of sub-section (3), the Chief Information Commissioner or any Information Commissioner shall be removed from his office only by order of the President on the ground of proved misbehaviour or incapacity after the Supreme Court, on a reference made to it by the President, has, on inquiry, reported that the Chief Information Commissioner or any Information Commissioner, as the case may be, ought on such ground be removed.

(2) The President may suspend from office, and if deem necessary prohibit also from attending the office during inquiry, the Chief Information Commissioner or Information Commissioner in respect of whom a reference has been made to the Supreme Court under sub-section (1) until the President has passed orders on receipt of the report of the Supreme Court on such reference.

(3) Notwithstanding anything contained in sub-section (1), the President may by order remove from office the Chief Information Commissioner or any Information Commissioner if the Chief Information Commissioner or a Information Commissioner, as the case may be,—

(a) is adjudged an insolvent; or

(b) has been convicted of an offence which, in the opinion of the President, involves moral turpitude; or

(c) engages during his term of office in any paid employment outside the duties of his office; or

(d) is, in the opinion of the President, unfit to continue in office by reason of infirmity of mind or body; or

(e) has acquired such financial or other interest as is likely to affect prejudicially his functions as the Chief Information Commissioner or a Information Commissioner.

(4) If the Chief Information Commissioner or a Information Commissioner in any way, concerned or interested in any contract or agreement made by or on behalf of the Government of India or participates in any way in the profit thereof or in any benefit or emolument arising there from otherwise than as a member and in common with the other members of an incorporated company, he shall, for the purposes of sub-section (1), be deemed to be guilty of misbehavior.

CHAPTER - IV : THE STATE INFORMATION COMMISSION

15. (1) Every State Government shall, by notification in the Official Gazette, constitute a body to be known as the .... (name of the State) Information Commission to exercise the powers conferred on, and to perform the functions assigned to, it under this Act.

(2) The State Information Commission shall consist of—

(a) the State Chief Information Commissioner, and

(b) such number of State Information Commissioners, not exceeding ten, as may be deemed necessary.

(3) The State Chief Information Commissioner and the State Information Commissioners shall be appointed by the Governor on the recommendation of a committee consisting of—

(i) the Chief Minister, who shall be the Chairperson of the committee;

(ii) the Leader of Opposition in the Legislative Assembly; and

(iii) a Cabinet Minister to be nominated by the Chief Minister.

Explanation.—For the purposes of removal of doubts, it is hereby declared that where the Leader of Opposition in the Legislative Assembly has not been recognised as such, the Leader of the single largest group in opposition of the Government in the Legislative Assembly shall be deemed to be the Leader of Opposition.

(4) The general superintendence, direction and management of the affairs of the State Information Commission shall vest in the State Chief Information Commissioner who shall be assisted by the State Information Commissioners and may exercise all such powers and do all such acts and things which may be exercised or done by the State Information Commission autonomously without being subjected to directions by any other authority under this Act.

(5) The State Chief Information Commissioner and the State Information Commissioners shall be persons of eminence in public life with wide knowledge and experience in law, science and technology, social service, management, journalism, mass media or administration and governance.

(6) The State Chief Information Commissioner or a State Information Commissioner shall not be a Member of Parliament or Member of the Legislature of any State or Union territory, as the case may be, or hold any other office of profit or connected with any political party or carrying on any business or pursuing any profession.

(7) The headquarters of the State Information Commission shall be at such place in the State as the State Government may, by notification in the Official Gazette, specify and the State Information Commission may, with the previous approval of the State Government, establish offices at other places in the State.

16. (1) The State Chief Information Commissioner shall hold office for a term of five years from the date on which he enters upon his office and shall not be eligible for reappointment:

Provided that no State Chief Information Commissioner shall hold office as such after he has attained the age of sixty-five years.

(2) Every State Information Commissioner shall hold office for a term of five years from the date on which he enters upon his office or till he attains the age of sixty-five years, whichever is earlier, and shall not be eligible for reappointment as such State Information Commissioner:

Provided that every State Information Commissioner shall, on vacating his office under this sub-section, be eligible for appointment as the State Chief Information Commissioner in the manner specified in sub-section (3) of section 15:

Provided further that where the State Information Commissioner is appointed as the State Chief Information Commissioner, his term of office shall not be more than five years in aggregate as the State Information Commissioner and the State Chief Information Commissioner.

(3) The State Chief Information Commissioner or a State Information Commissioner, shall before he enters upon his office make and subscribe before the Governor or some other person appointed by him in that behalf, an oath or affirmation according to the form set out for the purpose in the First Schedule.

(4) The State Chief Information Commissioner or a State Information Commissioner may, at any time, by writing under his hand addressed to the Governor, resign from his office:

Provided that the State Chief Information Commissioner or a State Information Commissioner may be removed in the manner specified under section 17.

(5) The salaries and allowances payable to and other terms and conditions of service of—

(a) the State Chief Information Commissioner shall be the same as that of an Election Commissioner;

(b) the State Information Commissioner shall be the same as that of the Chief Secretary to the State Government:

Provided that if the State Chief Information Commissioner or a State Information Commissioner, at the time of his appointment is, in receipt of a pension, other than a disability or wound pension, in respect of any previous service under the Government of India or under the Government of a State, his salary in respect of the service as the State Chief Information Commissioner or a State Information Commissioner shall be reduced by the amount of that pension including any portion of pension which was commuted and pension equivalent of other forms of retirement benefits excluding pension equivalent of retirement gratuity:

Provided further that where the State Chief Information Commissioner or a State Information Commissioner if, at the time of his appointment is, in receipt of retirement benefits in respect of any previous service rendered in a Corporation established by or under any Central Act or State Act or a Government company owned or controlled by the Central Government or the State Government, his salary in respect of the service as the State Chief Information Commissioner or the State Information Commissioner shall be reduced by the amount of pension equivalent to the retirement benefits:

Provided also that the salaries, allowances and other conditions of service of the State Chief Information Commissioner and the State Information Commissioners shall not be varied to their disadvantage after their appointment.

(6) The State Government shall provide the State Chief Information Commissioner and the State Information Commissioners with such officers and employees as may be necessary for the efficient performance of their functions under this Act, and the salaries and allowances payable to and the terms and conditions of service of the officers and other employees appointed for the purpose of this Act shall be such as may be prescribed.

17. (1) Subject to the provisions of sub-section (3), the State Chief Information Commissioner or a State Information Commissioner shall be removed from his office only by order of the Governor on the ground of proved misbehaviour or incapacity after the Supreme Court, on a reference made to it by the Governor, has on inquiry, reported that the State Chief Information Commissioner or a State Information Commissioner, as the case may be, ought on such ground be removed.

(2) The Governor may suspend from office, and if deem necessary prohibit also from attending the office during inquiry, the State Chief Information Commissioner or a State Information Commissioner in respect of whom a reference has been made to the Supreme Court under sub-section (1) until the Governor has passed orders on receipt of the report of the Supreme Court on such reference.

(3) Notwithstanding anything contained in sub-section (1), the Governor may by order remove from office the State Chief Information Commissioner or a State Information

Commissioner if a State Chief Information Commissioner or a State Information Commissioner, as the case may be,—

(a) is adjudged an insolvent; or

(b) has been convicted of an offence which, in the opinion of the Governor, involves moral turpitude; or

(c) engages during his term of office in any paid employment outside the duties of his office; or

(d) is, in the opinion of the Governor, unfit to continue in office by reason of infirmity of mind or body; or

(e) has acquired such financial or other interest as is likely to affect prejudicially his functions as the State Chief Information Commissioner or a State Information Commissioner.

(4) If the State Chief Information Commissioner or a State Information Commissioner in any way, concerned or interested in any contract or agreement made by or on behalf of the Government of the State or participates in any way in the profit thereof or in any benefit or emoluments arising therefrom otherwise than as a member and in common with the other members of an incorporated company, he shall, for the purposes of sub-section (1), be deemed to be guilty of misbehaviour.

CHAPTER - V : POWERS AND FUNCTIONS OF THE INFORMATION COMMISSIONS, APPEAL AND PENALTIES

18. (1) Subject to the provisions of this Act, it shall be the duty of the Central Information Commission or State Information Commission, as the case may be, to receive and inquire into a complaint from any person,—

(a) who has been unable to submit a request to a Central Public Information Officer or State Public Information Officer, as the case may be, either by reason that no such officer has been appointed under this Act, or because the Central Assistant Public Information Officer or State Assistant Public Information Officer, as the case may be, has refused to accept his or her application for information or appeal under this Act for forwarding the same to the Central Public Information Officer or State Public Information Officer or senior officer specified in sub-section (1) of section 19 or the Central Information Commission or the State Information Commission, as the case may be;

(b) who has been refused access to any information requested under this Act;

(c) who has not been given a response to a request for information or access to information within the time limit specified under this Act;

(d) who has been required to pay an amount of fee which he or she considers unreasonable;

(e) who believes that he or she has been given incomplete, misleading or false information under this Act; and

(f) in respect of any other matter relating to requesting or obtaining access to records under this Act.

(2) Where the Central Information Commission or State Information Commission, as the case may be, is satisfied that there are reasonable grounds to inquire into the matter, it may initiate an inquiry in respect thereof.

(3). The Central Information Commission or State Information Commission, as the case may be, shall, while inquiring into any matter under this section, have the same powers as are vested in a civil court while trying a suit under the Code of Civil Procedure, 1908, in respect of the following matters, namely:—

(a) summoning and enforcing the attendance of persons and compel them to give oral or written evidence on oath and to produce the documents or things;

(b) requiring the discovery and inspection of documents;

(c) receiving evidence on affidavit;

(d) requisitioning any public record or copies thereof from any court or office;

(e) issuing summons for examination of witnesses or documents; and

(f) any other matter which may be prescribed.

(4) Notwithstanding anything inconsistent contained in any other Act of Parliament or State Legislature, as the case may be, the Central Information Commission or the State Information Commission, as the case may be, may, during the inquiry of any complaint under this Act, examine any record to which this Act applies which is under the control of the public authority, and no such record may be withheld from it on any grounds.

19. (1) Any person who, does not receive a decision within the time specified in sub-section (1) or clause (a) of sub-section (3) of section 7, or is aggrieved by a decision of the Central Public Information Officer or State Public Information Officer, as the case may be, may within thirty days from the expiry of such period or from the receipt of such a decision prefer an appeal to such officer who is senior in rank to the Central Public Information Officer or State Public Information Officer as the case may be, in each public authority:

Provided that such officer may admit the appeal after the expiry of the period of thirty days if he or she is satisfied that the appellant was prevented by sufficient cause from filing the appeal in time.

(2) Where an appeal is preferred against an order made by a Central Public Information Officer or a State Public Information Officer, as the case may be, under section 11 to disclose third party information, the appeal by the concerned third party shall be made within thirty days from the date of the order.

(3) A second appeal against the decision under sub-section (1) shall lie within ninety days from the date on which the decision should have been made or was actually received, with the Central Information Commission or the State Information Commission:

Provided that the Central Information Commission or the State Information Commission, as the case may be, may admit the appeal after the expiry of the period of ninety days if it is satisfied that the appellant was prevented by sufficient cause from filing the appeal in time.

(4) If the decision of the Central Public Information Officer or State Public Information Officer, as the case may be, against which an appeal is preferred relates to information of a third party, the Central Information Commission or State Information Commission, as the case may be, shall give a reasonable opportunity of being heard to that third party.

(5) In any appeal proceedings, the onus to prove that a denial of a request was justified shall be on the Central Public Information Officer or State Public Information Officer, as the case may be, who denied the request.

(6) An appeal under sub-section (1) or sub-section (2) shall be disposed of within thirty days of the receipt of the appeal or within such extended period not exceeding a total of forty-five days from the date of filing thereof, as the case may be, for reasons to be recorded in writing.

(7) The decision of the Central Information Commission or State Information Commission, as the case may be, shall be binding.

(8) In its decision, the Central Information Commission or State Information Commission, as the case may be, has the power to—

(a) require the public authority to take any such steps as may be necessary to secure compliance with the provisions of this Act, including—

(i) by providing access to information, if so requested, in a particular form;

(ii) by appointing a Central Public Information Officer or State Public Information Officer, as the case may be;

(iii) by publishing certain information or categories of information;

(iv) by making necessary changes to its practices in relation to the maintenance, management and destruction of records;

(v) by enhancing the provision of training on the right to information for its officials;

(vi) by providing it with an annual report in compliance with clause (b) of sub-section (1) of section 4;

(b) require the public authority to compensate the complainant for any loss or other detriment suffered;

(c) impose any of the penalties provided under this Act;

(d) reject the application.

(9) The Central Information Commission or State Information Commission, as the case may be, shall give notice of its decision, including any right of appeal, to the complainant and the public authority.

(10) The Central Information Commission or State Information Commission, as the case may be, shall decide the appeal in accordance with such procedure as may be prescribed.

20. (1) Where the Central Information Commission or the State Information Commission, as the case may be, at the time of deciding any complaint or appeal is of the opinion that the Central Public Information Officer or the State Public Information Officer, as the case may be, has, without any reasonable cause, refused to receive an application for information or has not furnished information within the time specified under sub-section (1) of section 7 or malafidely denied the request for information or knowingly given incorrect, incomplete or misleading information or destroyed information which was the subject of the request or obstructed in any manner in furnishing the information, it shall impose a penalty of two hundred and fifty rupees each day till application is received or information is furnished, so however, the total amount of such penalty shall not exceed twenty-five thousand rupees:

Provided that the Central Public Information Officer or the State Public Information Officer, as the case may be, shall be given a reasonable opportunity of being heard before any penalty is imposed on him:

Provided further that the burden of proving that he acted reasonably and diligently shall be on the Central Public Information Officer or the State Public Information Officer, as the case may be.

(2) Where the Central Information Commission or the State Information Commission, as the case may be, at the time of deciding any complaint or appeal is of the opinion that the Central Public Information Officer or the State Public Information Officer, as the case may be, has, without any reasonable cause and persistently, failed to receive an application for information or has not furnished information within the time specified under sub-section (1) of section 7 or malafidely denied the request for information or knowingly given incorrect, incomplete or misleading information or destroyed information which was the subject of the request or obstructed in any manner in furnishing the information, it shall recommend for disciplinary action against the Central Public Information Officer or the State Public Information Officer, as the case may be, under the service rules applicable to him.

CHAPTER - VI : MISCELLANEOUS

21. No suit, prosecution or other legal proceeding shall lie against any person for anything which is in good faith done or intended to be done under this Act or any rule made thereunder.

22. The provisions of this Act shall have effect notwithstanding anything inconsistent therewith contained in the Official Secrets Act, 1923, and any other law for the time being in force or in any instrument having effect by virtue of any law other than this Act.

23. No court shall entertain any suit, application or other proceeding in respect of any order made under this Act and no such order shall be called in question otherwise than by way of an appeal under this Act.

24. (1) Nothing contained in this Act shall apply to the intelligence and security organisations specified in the Second Schedule, being organisations established by the Central Government or any information furnished by such organisations to that Government:

Provided that the information pertaining to the allegations of corruption and human rights violations shall not be excluded under this sub-section:

Provided further that in the case of information sought for is in respect of allegations of violation of human rights, the information shall only be provided after the approval of the Central Information Commission, and notwithstanding anything contained in section 7, such information shall be provided within forty-five days from the date of the receipt of request.

(2) The Central Government may, by notification in the Official Gazette, amend the Schedule by including therein any other intelligence or security organisation established by that Government or omitting therefrom any organisation already specified therein and on the publication of such notification, such organisation shall be deemed to be included in or, as the case may be, omitted from the Schedule.

(3) Every notification issued under sub-section (2) shall be laid before each House of Parliament.

(4) Nothing contained in this Act shall apply to such intelligence and security organisation being organisations established by the State Government, as that Government may, from time to time, by notification in the Official Gazette, specify:

Provided that the information pertaining to the allegations of corruption and human rights violations shall not be excluded under this sub-section:

Provided further that in the case of information sought for is in respect of allegations of violation of human rights, the information shall only be provided after the approval of the State Information Commission and, notwithstanding anything contained in section 7, such information shall be provided within forty-five days from the date of the receipt of request.

(5) Every notification issued under sub-section (4) shall be laid before the State Legislature.

25. (1) The Central Information Commission or State Information Commission, as the case may be, shall, as soon as practicable after the end of each year, prepare a report on the implementation of the provisions of this Act during that year and forward a copy thereof to the appropriate Government.

(2) Each Ministry or Department shall, in relation to the public authorities within their jurisdiction, collect and provide such information to the Central Information Commission or State Information Commission, as the case may be, as is required to prepare the report under this section and comply with the requirements concerning the furnishing of that information and keeping of records for the purposes of this section.

(3) Each report shall state in respect of the year to which the report relates,—

(a) the number of requests made to each public authority;

(b) the number of decisions where applicants were not entitled to access to the documents pursuant to the requests, the provisions of this Act under which these decisions were made and the number of times such provisions were invoked;

(c) the number of appeals referred to the Central Information Commission or State Information Commission, as the case may be, for review, the nature of the appeals and the outcome of the appeals;

(d) particulars of any disciplinary action taken against any officer in respect of the administration of this Act;

(e) the amount of charges collected by each public authority under this Act;

(f) any facts which indicate an effort by the public authorities to administer and implement the spirit and intention of this Act;

(g) recommendations for reform, including recommendations in respect of the particular public authorities, for the development, improvement, modernisation, reform or amendment to this Act or other legislation or common law or any other matter relevant for operationalising the right to access information.

(4) The Central Government or the State Government, as the case may be, may, as soon as practicable after the end of each year, cause a copy of the report of the Central Information Commission or the State Information Commission, as the case may be, referred to in sub-section (1) to be laid before each House of Parliament or, as the case may be, before each House of the State Legislature, where there are two Houses, and where there is one House of the State Legislature before that House.

(5) If it appears to the Central Information Commission or State Information Commission, as the case may be, that the practice of a public authority in relation to the exercise of its functions under this Act does not conform with the provisions or spirit of this Act, it may give to the authority a recommendation specifying the steps which ought in its opinion to be taken for promoting such conformity.

26. (1) The appropriate Government may, to the extent of availability of financial and other resources,—

(a) develop and organise educational programmes to advance the understanding of the public, in particular of disadvantaged communities as to how to exercise the rights contemplated under this Act;

(b) encourage public authorities to participate in the development and organisation of programmes referred to in clause (a) and to undertake such programmes themselves;

(c) promote timely and effective dissemination of accurate information by public authorities about their activities; and

(d) train Central Public Information Officers or State Public Information Officers, as the case may be, of public authorities and produce relevant training materials for use by the public authorities themselves.

(2) The appropriate Government shall, within eighteen months from the commencement of this Act, compile in its official language a guide containing such information, in an easily comprehensible form and manner, as may reasonably be required by a person who wishes to exercise any right specified in this Act.

(3) The appropriate Government shall, if necessary, update and publish the guidelines referred to in sub-section (2) at regular intervals which shall, in particular and without prejudice to the generality of sub-section (2), include—

(a) the objects of this Act;

(b) the postal and street address, the phone and fax number and, if available, electronic mail address of the Central Public Information Officer or State Public Information Officer, as the case may be, of every public authority appointed under sub-section (1) of section 5;

(c) the manner and the form in which request for access to an information shall be made to a Central Public Information Officer or State Public Information Officer, as the case may be;

(d) the assistance available from and the duties of the Central Public Information Officer or State Public Information Officer, as the case may be, of a public authority under this Act;

(e) the assistance available from the Central Information Commission or State Information Commission, as the case may be;

(f) all remedies in law available regarding an act or failure to act in respect of a right or duty conferred or imposed by this Act including the manner of filing an appeal to the Commission;

(g) the provisions providing for the voluntary disclosure of categories of records in accordance with section 4;

(h) the notices regarding fees to be paid in relation to requests for access to an information; and

(i) any additional regulations or circulars made or issued in relation to obtaining access to an information in accordance with this Act.

(4) The appropriate Government must, if necessary, update and publish the guidelines at regular intervals.

27. (1) The appropriate Government may, by notification in the Official Gazette, make rules to carry out the provisions of this Act.

(2) In particular, and without prejudice to the generality of the foregoing power, such rules may provide for all or any of the following matters, namely:—

(a) the cost of the medium or print cost price of the materials to be disseminated under sub-section (4) of section 4;

(b) the fee payable under sub-section (1) of section 6;

(c) the fee payable under sub-sections (1) and (5) of section 7;

(d) the salaries and allowances payable to and the terms and conditions of service of the officers and other employees under sub-section (6) of section 13 and sub-section (6) of section 16;

(e) the procedure to be adopted by the Central Information Commission or State Information Commission, as the case may be, in deciding the appeals under sub-section (10) of section 19; and

(f) any other matter which is required to be, or may be, prescribed.

28 (1) The competent authority may, by notification in the Official Gazette, make rules to carry out the provisions of this Act.

(2) In particular, and without prejudice to the generality of the foregoing power, such rules may provide for all or any of the following matters, namely:—

(i) the cost of the medium or print cost price of the materials to be disseminated under sub-section (4) of section 4;

(ii) the fee payable under sub-section (1) of section 6;

(iii) the fee payable under sub-section (1) of section 7; and

(iv) any other matter which is required to be, or may be, prescribed.

29. (1) Every rule made by the Central Government under this Act shall be laid, as soon as may be after it is made, before each House of Parliament, while it is in session, for a total period of thirty days which may be comprised in one session or in two or more successive sessions, and if, before the expiry of the session immediately following the session or the successive sessions aforesaid, both Houses agree in making any modification in the rule or both Houses agree that the rule should not be made, the rule shall thereafter have effect only in such modified form or be of no effect, as the case may be; so, however, that any such modification or annulment shall be without prejudice to the validity of anything previously done under that rule.

(2) Every rule made under this Act by a State Government shall be laid, as soon as may be after it is notified, before the State Legislature.

30. (1) If any difficulty arises in giving effect to the provisions of this Act, the Central Government may, by order published in the Official Gazette, make such provisions not inconsistent with the provisions of this Act as appear to it to be necessary or expedient for removal of the difficulty:

Provided that no such order shall be made after the expiry of a period of two years from the date of the commencement of this Act.

(2) Every order made under this section shall, as soon as may be after it is made, be laid before each House of Parliament.

31. The Freedom of Information Act, 2002 is hereby repealed.

THE FIRST SCHEDULE

[*See* sections 13(3) and 16(3)]

Form of oath or affirmation to be made by the Chief Information Commissioner/the Information Commissioner/the State Chief Information Commissioner/the State Information Commissioner

"I, ..., having been appointed Chief Information Commissioner/Information Commissioner/State Chief Information Commissioner/State Information Commissioner .... swear in the name of God .... solemnly affirm that I will bear true faith and allegiance to the Constitution of India as by law established, that I will uphold the sovereignty and integrity of India, that I will duly and faithfully and to the best of my ability, knowledge and judgment perform the duties of my office without fear or favour, affection or ill-will and that I will uphold the Constitution and the laws.".

THE SECOND SCHEDULE

(*See* section 24)

Intelligence and security organisation established by the Central Government

1. Intelligence Bureau.
2. Research and Analysis Wing of the Cabinet Secretariat.
3. Directorate of Revenue Intelligence.
4. Central Economic Intelligence Bureau.
5. Directorate of Enforcement.
6. Narcotics Control Bureau.
7. Aviation Research Centre.
8. Special Frontier Force.
9. Border Security Force.
10. Central Reserve Police Force.
11. Indo-Tibetan Border Police.
12. Central Industrial Security Force.
13. National Security Guards.
14. Assam Rifles.
15. Special Service Bureau.
16. Special Branch (CID), Andaman and Nicobar.
17. The Crime Branch-C.I.D.- CB, Dadra and Nagar Haveli.
18. Special Branch, Lakshadweep Police.

❑❑❑

5

Awards and Honours to Anna Hazare

Introduction

Anna Hazare has been honoured with the Padma Shri in 1990 and the Padma Vibhushan in 1992. In addition, he has been the recipient of numerous awards from various state, national and international organizations, including the prestigious Transparency International (IT) Integrity award in 2003 from Transparency International.

AWARDS TO ANNA HAZARE

PADMABHUSHAN AWARD

It is presented by R. Venkatraman (President of India) on 6th April 1992 at Delhi for Anna Hazare's social work. Padma Awards, namely, **Padma Vibhushan, Padma Bhushan** and **Padma Shri** are given for exceptional and distinguished service in any field including service rendered by Government servants. The recommendations for Padma Awards are received from the State Governments/Union Territory Administrations, Central Ministries/Departments, Institutions of Excellence, etc. which are considered by an Awards

Committee. On the basis of the recommendations of the Awards Committee, and after approval of the Home Minister, Prime Minister and President, the Padma Awards are announced on the eve of the Republic Day.

PADMASHRI AWARD

It is presented by R. Venkatraman (President of India) on 24th march 1990 at Delhi for Anna Hazare's social work.

PRIY DARSHINI VRIKSHA MITRA AWARD, GOVT. INDIA

The Key features are:-a) Award of Rs. 2,50,000/- (Two lakhs fifty thousands only) in cash alongwith medallions and citations will be given to persons/institutions in *four* categories. Nominations for the works in the field of afforestation and wasteland development will be considered and assessed on the basis of criteria like replicability, innovativeness/ creativity, setting up of grass root level organizations, soil and moisture conservation work and other related activities, targets groups like women/weaker sections of society, people in accessible/ remote areas, work being done over and above the call of duty/involving personal courage, tangible impact in relation to resources mobilized, educative and awareness creating values etc.

The nominations from Government Servants, Institutions / Organizations under Government should be sponsored by the concerned State Governments/ Government Agencies and should be forwarded by the Head of the Department/ Institution/ Organization with his/her comments and sent to the Principal Chief Conservator of Forest of the concerned State for overall assessment.

The nominations of Joint Forest Management Committees, Non-government Institutions/ Organizations/ Individuals should be sponsored by the concerned State Governments/ Government Agencies/ Registered NGOs and should be sent to the Principal Chief Conservator of Forest of the concerned State for overall assessment. An awardee of IPVM award in the immediately preceding three years will not be eligible.

An applicant may receive a maximum of three IPVM awards altogether in any of the categories taken together with a minimum cooling off period of three years between the two awards. Nominee's work for a period of last three years ending 31st December of the preceding year will be considered for this award. Nominations with predominance of horticulture species will be regarded as eligible since horticulture species have a definite commercial slant.

In case of Corporate Sector, the extent of mandatory plantation to be done by the applicants under compensatory afforestation or under the provision of the Environment Protection Act shall be separately ascertained and excluded from the area of plantation for consideration of award. Tree planting undertaken purely on commercial basis by applicant including Corporate Sector will not be regarded as eligible for consideration for the award. The tree planting activity should clearly reflect the social responsibility of the applicant including that of the Corporate Sector, i) Special recognition will be given to applicants who bring area with fly ash under the plantation, Applications under the following conditions will be rendered ineligible:

a. Nomination not forwarded/ sponsored as prescribed in para(c) above will not be considered.
b. Nominations not received in prescribed proforma/ incomplete in any respect and/or received after the last date will not be considered.
c. Applicants found to be suppressing information or giving false and misleading information would be disqualified for grant of IPVM or any other award of the Ministry.

YOUNG INDIA AWARD

In recognition of outstanding services to the community, Young India is awarded National Youth Award. Since 1989 Young India has taken commendable steps in the field of youth development, promotion of local self governance, gender equality, human rights etc. Thousands of youth are trained in different capacity building trainings organised by Young India. A number of unique & innovative steps are also taken by Young India which are well visible in the country. Since International Year of Volunteers 2001 Young India has been organising a national level youth congregation at

Konark, Orissa entitles "Konark Youth Fest". To engender database of Indian Volunteers & promote networking among them for exchange of Knowledge, Expertise, ideas & information Young India has also started a volunteers portal i.e. www.volunteersindia.in which is the only such type portal in the country. Young India has also established Radio Namaskar (FM 90.4 MHz) the only community radio of Orissa to promote voice of the voiceless. For such types of actions Young India is awarded which has shown a new light to the youth population of the country.

Apart from these awards there are various awards given to him on various occasions. The awards and Prizes are given below:-

MAN OF THE YEAR AWARD 1988

PAUL MITTAL NATIONAL AWARD 2000 (NEHRU SIDHANT KENDER TRUST LUDHIYNA 14001)

It is presented by shri. Balaramji Das Tandon (Minister, Punjab) on 14th november 2000.

TRANSPARENCY INTERNATIONAL (IT) INTEGRITY AWARD 2003 FROM TRANSPARENCY INTERNATIONAL

DOCTORATE DEGREE GANDHIGRAM RURAL INSTITUTE-DEEMED UNIVERSITY GANDHIGRAM DINDIGUL, TAMIL NADU-8-11-05

VIVEKANANDA SEVA PURASKAR 1994

It is presented by Shri.Bada Bajar Kumar Sabha Pustakalay, Calcutta on 12th June 1996 for Anna Hazare's social work done for develop village as a family.

SHIROMANI AWARD 1996

It is presented by P. A. Sangma (Speaker of Lok sabha) on 22nd February 1997 at New Delhi for Anna Hazare's contribution to National Development Integration, Enrichment of life and for his outstanding achievements in the choosen field of activities(social service).

MAHAVEER PURASKAR 1997

It is presented by Bhagwan Mahaveer Foundation , Chennai on 2th April 1997 for Anna Hazare's excellent in sphere of social & community service.

DIWALIBEN MEHTA AWARD

It is presented by Shri.Panduranga Shastri Athavale on 8th January 1999 at Mumbai for Anna Hazare's Hard, Sincere, Dedicated & Devoted social work.

CARE INTERNATIONAL AWARD 1998

It is presented by Care International Humanitarian on 8th May 1998 at Washington, D.C, USA for Anna Hazare demonstrating a profound commitment to improving life in developing world. Care Recognized Anna Hazare's devotion to the ideas of sustainable development with whole hearted participation of villagers including women & youth.

GIANTS INTERNATIONAL AWARD

It is presented by Shri.Vilas Rao Deshmukh (Chief Minister of Maharashtra) on 17th sept. 2000 for Shri.Anna hazare's social work

BASAVSHRI PRASHASTI 2000 AWARD

It is presented by Shri. Jagadguru Murugharajendra Brihan Math at S.J.M.Math, Chitradurga , Karnataka on 4th June 2000 for Anna Hazare's relentless effort to bring in the value of based way of life in the society.

NATIONAL INTERGRATION AWARD

It is presented by (Dhum-Lajee) chief minister- Himothkursh Sahithy Samskruthi Avam Jana Kalyal Parishad, UNA, Himachal Pradesh on 14th February 1999 for Anna Hazare's Social Work.

VISHWA-VATSALYA & SANTBAL AWARD

It is presented at Ahamadabad for Anna Hazares universal services to mankind including his incessant fight against corruption and his inspring efforts to improve the living condition of the poor & to ri\aise the ethical levels of the society.

JANA SEVA PURASKAR

It is presented by Smt. Rajmathi at Sangle, Maharashtra on 28th February 1998 for Anna Hazares Social Work.

ROTARY INTERNATIONAL MANAV SEVA PURASKAR

It is presented by Supreme Court Judge Shri. D.P. Wadhwa at India Habital Center, Lodhi Road, New Delhi on 21st Feb 1998 for Anna Hazare's Crusade against Corruption .

Felicitations

He was felicitated by the Ahmednagar Municipal Corporation on 15 January 1987 and by the Pune Municipal Corporation.

6

Lokpal Bill by Government of India

The Lok Bill, 2010

A BILL to provide for the establishment of the institution of Lokpal to inquire into allegations of corruption against public functionaries and for matters connected therewith.

BE it enacted by parliament in the Sixty-first Year of the Republic of India as follows:-

CHAPTER - 1 : PRELIMINARY

1. Short title and commencement.

(1) This Act may be called the Lokpal Act, 2010.

(2) It shall come into force on such date as the central Government may, by notification in the official Gazette, appoint.

2. Definitions. In this Act, unless the context otherwise requires,-

(1) "Chairperson" means the Chairperson of the Lokpal;

(2) "competent authority", in relation to –

(i) the Prime Minister, means the house of the people;

(ii) a member of the Council of Ministers, other than the Prime Minister, means the Prime Ministers; and

(iii) a member of Parliament, other than a Minister means the Council of states in the case of a member of that Council and the House of the people in the case of a member of that House;

(3) "memorandum of complaints" means a memorandum of complaints alleging that a public functionary has committed any offence punishable under the prevention of corruption Act, 1988;

(4) "inquiry" means every inquiry conducted under this Act by the Lokpal;

(5) "Lokpal" means the institution established under section 3;

(6) "Member" means a Member of the Lokpal;

(7) "prescribed" means prescribed by rules made under this Act;

(8) "public functionary" means a person who-

(i) Holds or has held the office of the prime Minister. Minister, Minister of state or Deputy Minister of the Union; or

(ii) is or has been a member of either House of Parliament.

CHAPTER - II : MACHINARY FOR INQUIRIES

3. Establishment of Lokpal.

(1) As from the commencement of this Act, there shall be established, for the purpose of making inquires in respect of memorandum of complaints under this Act, an institution to be called the "Lokpal"

(2) The Lokpal shall consist of –

(i) a Chairperson who is or has been a chief justice or a judge of the Supreme Court; and

(ii) two Members who are or have been the judge of the Supreme court or the chief justices of the High courts.

(3) The chairperson and every other member shall, before entering upon his office, make and subscribe before the president , or a person appointed in that behalf by the president, an oath or affirmation in the form set out in the Schedule.

4. Appointment of Chairperson and members.

(1) The chairperson and member shall be appointed by the President by warrant under his hand and seal:

(2) Every appointment under sub-section (1) shall be made after obtaining the recommendations of a committee consisting of—

The vice-president of India	Chairman;
The Prime Minister	-member;
The speaker of the House of the People	-member;
The Minister in charge of the Ministry of Home affairs in the Government of India	-member;
The Minister in-charge of the Ministry of Law and justice in the Government of India	-member;
The Leader of the House other than the House in which the prime Minister is a member of Parliament	-member;
The Leader of the Opposition in the house of the people	-member;
The leader of the opposition in the council of States	-member;

Provided that in case, there is no ledger of opposition in the house of the people or the council of states, the leader of the single largest group or party in opposition to the government, as the case may be, in such House or council shall be deemed to be a member of the committee specified in clause (g) or clause (h), as the case may be:

Provide further that no sitting judge of the Supreme court or sitting Chief justice of a High court shall be appointed except after consultation with the chief justice of India.

(3) No appointment of a chairperson or a member shall be invalid merely by reason of any vacancy in the committee.

5. Chairperson and members to be ineligible to hold other office. The Chairperson or a member shall not be a member of parliament or a member of the legislature of any state or union territory and shall not hold any office of trust or profit (other than his office as the chairperson or a member) or be connected with any political party or carry on any business or practice any profession and accordingly, before he enters upon his office, a person appointed as the chairperson or a Member , as the case may be, shall, if –

- He is a member of parliament or of the legislature of any state or Union territory, resign such membership; or
- He holds any office of trust or profit, resign from such office, or
- He is connected with any political party , server his connection with it; or
- He is carrying on any business , server his connection (short of divesting himself of ownership) with the conduct and management of such business; or
- He is practicing any profession, cease to practice such profession.

6. Term of office and other conditions of service of chairperson and member.

(1) The chairperson and every other member shall hold office as such for a term of three years from the date on which he enters upon his office or until he attains the age of seventy years, whichever is earlier:

Provided that he may –

(a) By writing under his hand addressed to the president, resign his office; or

(b) Be removed from his office in the manner provided in section 7.

(2) On ceasing to hold office , the chairperson and every other member shall be ineligible for –

(i) Reappointment in the Lokpal;

(ii) any diplomatic assignment, appointment as administrator of a Union territory and such other assignment or appointment which is required by law to be made by the president by warrant under his hand and seal; and

(iii) further employment to any other office of profit under the Government of India or the Government of a State

(3) The salary, allowances and other conditions of service of –

(i) the chairperson shall be the same as those of the chief justice of India;

(ii) other members shall be the same as those of a judge of the Supreme court:

Provided that if the chairperson or a member is, at the time of his appointment, in receipt of a pension (other than a disability or would pension) in respect of any previous service under the government of India or under the government of a state, his salary in respect of service as the chairperson or, as the case may be, as a member, be reduced –

(i) By the amount of that pension; and

(ii) If he has, before such appointment, received, in lieu of a portion of the pension due to him in respect of such previous service, the commuted value thereof, by the amount of that portion of the pension:

Provided further that the salary, allowances and pension payable to, and other conditions of service of, the chairperson or a member shall not be varied to his disadvantage after his appointment.

7. Removal of chairperson or member. The chairperson or a member shall not be removed from his office except by an order made by the president on the ground of proved misbehavior or incapacity after an enquiry made by a committee consisting of the chief justice of India and two other judges of the supreme court next to the chief justice in seniority, in which the chairperson or the member had been informed of the charges against him and given a reasonable opportunity of being heard in respect of those charges.

8. Member reason as chairperson or to discharge his.

(1) In the event of the occurrence of any vacancy in the office of the chairperson by reason of his death resignation or otherwise the president may by notification authorise the senior -most member to act as the chairperson until the appointment of a new chairperson to fill such vacancy

(2) When the chairperson is unable to discharge his functions owing to absence on leave or otherwise the Senior most member available as the president may by notification authorise in this behalf shall discharge the functions of the chairperson until the date on which the chairperson resumes his duties

9. Staff of Lokpal.

(1) The Lokpal shall for the purpose of assisting it in the discharge of its functions (including verification and inquiries in respect of memorandum of complaints) under this Act appoint of memorandum such other officer and employees as the president may determine from time to time in consultation with the Lokpal.

(2) Without prejudice to the provisions of sub- section (i) the Lokpal may for the purpose of dealing with any memorandum of complaints or any class of memorandum of complaints secure-

   (i) the services of officer or employee or investigating agency of the central government or a state government with the concurrence of the Government, or

   (ii) the services of any other person or Agency

(3) The terms and conditions of service of the Officers and employees referred to in sub -section (1) and of the officers employees agencies and persons referred to in sub- section (2)(including such special conditions as may be considered necessary for enabling them to act without fear or favour in the discharge of their functions) shall be such as the

president may determine from time to time in consultation the Lokpal.

(4) In the discharge of their functions under this act the officers and employees referred to in sub-section and the officer employees agencies and persons referred to on sub-section (2) shall be subject to the exclusive administrative control and direction of the Lokpal.

CHAPTER - III : JURISDICTION AND PROCEDURE IN RESPECT OF INQUIRIES

10. Jurisdiction of Lokpal

(1) Subject to the other provisions of this Act, the Lokpal shall enquire into any matter involved in, or arising from, or connected with, any allegation of corruption made in a memorandum of complaints:

Provided that the Lokpal shall not enquire into any matter involved in , or arising from, or connected with, any such allegation of corruption against the prime Minister in so far as it relates to national security, maintenance of public order, national defence and foreign relations:

Provided that Lokpal shall not inquire into any matter involved in, or arising from or connected with, any such allegation of corruption against any Member of either House of parliament unless the recommendation of the speaker of House of people or the chairmen of council of states, as the case may be, is received by it.

(2) The Lokpal may enquire into any Act or conduct of any person other than a public functionary in so far as it considers it necessary so to do for the purpose of its inquiry into any such allegation of corruption:

Provided that the Lokpal shall give such person a reasonable opportunity of being heard and to produce evidence in his defence.

(3) No matter in respect of which a memorandum of complaints may be made under this Act, shall be referred for inquiry under the commissions of inquiry Act, 1952.

11. Matters not subject to jurisdiction of Lokpal

(1) The Lokpal shall not inquire into any matter concerning any person if the Chairperson or any Member has any bias in respect of such matter or person and if any dispute arises in this behalf, the president shall, on an application made by the party aggrieved, obtain, in such manner as may be prescribed the opinion of the chief Justice of India and decide the dispute in conformity with such opinion.

(2) The Lokpal shall not inquire into any memorandum of complaints if the memorandum of complaints is made after the expiry of five years from the data on which the offence mentioned in such memorandum of complaints is alleged to have been committed.

12. Memorandum of Complaints.

(1) Any person other than a public servant may make a memorandum of complaints' under this Act to the Lokpal.

Provided that memorandum other a complaints in case of prime minister shall be made to the speaker of the house of people and the Lokpal shall consider only such memorandum of complaints as are referred to it by the speaker of the House of people:

Provided further that memorandum of complaints in case of minister of state or deputy minister of the union and member of either House of parliament shall be made to the Speaker of House of people or the chairman of council of states as the case may be and lokpal shall consider only such memorandum of complaints as are referred to it by the speaker of the house of people or the chairman of council of states as the case may be:

Explanation: For the purposes of this sub-section "public servant" means—

- Any person who is a member of a defiance service or of a civil service of the union or a State or of an all India service or holds any post connected with defiance or any civil post under the union or a state;
- Any person in the service or pay of a local authority a corporation established by or under a central

provincial or state Act or a government company as defined in section 617 of the companies Act 1956;

- Any person in the service of any other institution, concern or under taking which is established by or under a Central, provincial or State Act or which is controlled, or financed wholly or substantially by funds provided, directly by the Central Government or a State Government.

(2) The memorandum of complaints shall be in the presided form and shall set forth particulars or the offence alleged and shall be accompanied by such particulars and a corticated of deposit furnished under sub- section (3)or, if the complainant is under to make the deposit, an application for exemption from the requirement as to such deposit.

(3) The complainant shall deposit such sum of money in such manner and with such authority or agency as may be prescribed and the certificate for such deposit shall be furnished in the prescribed form.

(4) Notwithstanding anything contained in the forgoing sub-section any letter written to the Lokpal by a person in any jail or other place for insane persons may if treated as a memorandum of complaints made in accordance with the provisions of this section.

(5) Notwithstanding anything c obtained in the any other enactment, it shall be the duty of a police officer or other person in-charge of any jail or other place of custody or of any asylum or other place for insane persons to forward , without opening , any letter addressed to the Lokpal by a person imprisoned or detained in such jail place of custody asylum or other place to the Lokpal without delay.

13. Preliminary scrutiny of memorandum of complaints by Lokpal.

(1) If the Lokpal is satisfied, after considering a memorandum of complaints and after making such verification as it deems appropriate that

(a) the memorandum of complaints is not made within a period of five years as specified in sub-section (2) of section 11; or

(b) the memorandum of complaints is manifestly false and vexatious;

The Lokpal shall dismiss the memorandum of complaints after recording its reasons therefore and communicate the same to the complainant and to the competent authority.

(2) The purpose for verification in respect of a memorandum of complaints under sub-section (1) shell be such as the Lokpal deems appropriate in the circumstances of the case and in particular, the Lokpal may, if it deem it necessary so to do, call for the comments of the public functionary concerned.

14. Procedure in respect of inquiries

(1) If, after the consideration and verification under section 13 in respect of a memorandum of complaints, the Lokpal proposes to conduct any inquiry, it—

- Shall forthwith forward a copy of the memorandum of complaints to the competent authority;
- May make such orders as to the safe custody of documents relevant to the enquiry as it deems fit; and
- Shall at such time as it considers appropriate, forward a copy of the memorandum of complaints to the public functionary concerned as afford him an opportunity to represent his case.

(2) Every enquiry shall be conducted by the chairperson and the member sitting jointly and the place in which such inquiry is conducted shall be deemed to be an open court to which the public generally may have access so far as the same can continently contain them;

Provide that in exceptional circumstances and for reason to be recorded in writing, such inquiry may be conducted in camera.

(3) The Lokpal shall hold every such enquiry as expeditiously as possible and in any case complete the enquiry with in a period of six months from the date of receipt of the memorandum of complaints;

Provided that the lokpal may, for reason to be recorded in writing. Complete the enquiry with in a further period of six months.

(4) Save as aforesaid the procedure for conducting any such enquiry shall be such as the lokpal considers appropriate in the circumstances of the case.

15. Evidence.

(1) subject to provisions of this section, for the purpose of any inquiry (including the verification under section 13), the lokpal—

(a) may require any public servant or any other person who in its opinion, is able to furnish information or produce document or relevant to such inquiry to furnish any such information or produce ant such document; and

(b) shall have all the power of a civil court, under the court of civil procedure 1908, while trying a suit in respect of following matters, namely:-

- Summoning and enforcing the attendance of any person and examining him on oath;
- Requiring the discovery and production of any document;
- Receiving evidence on affidavits;
- Requisitioning any public record or copy thereof from any court or office;
- issuing commission for the examination of witnesses or documents;

  Provide that such commission, in case of a witness, shall be issued only where the witness, in the opinion of the lokpal, is not in a position to attend the proceeding before the lokpal; and

- such other matter as may prescribed.

(2) Any proceeding before the Lokpal shall be deemed to be judicial proceeding within the meaning of section 193 of the Indian penal code.

(3) No obligation to maintain secrecy or other restriction upon the disclosure of information obtained by or furnished to Government or any public servant whether imposed by any enactment or by any provision of low whatever, shall apply

to the discloser of information for the purpose of any inquiry (including the verification under section 13 under this Act.

(4) The government or any public servant shall not be entitled, in relation to any such enquiry or verification under section 13 to any such privilege in respect of the production of documents of the giving of evidence as is allowed by any enactment or by any provision of law whatever in legal proceedings.

Explanation: for the purpose of this section, "public servant" shall have the same meaning as is in section 21 of the Indian panel code.

16. Search and seizure.

(1) If the Lokpal has reason to believe that any document which, in its opinion, shall be useful for, or relevant to, any inquiry under this Act, are secreted in any place, it may authorize any officer any subordinate to it, or any officer of an investigating agency referred to in subsection (2) of section 9, to search for and to size such documents.

(2) If the Lokpal is satisfied that any document sized under sub section (1) would be evidence for the purpose of any inquiry under this act and that it would be necessary to retain the document in its custody, it may so retain the said document till the completion of such inquiry;

Provide that where any document is required to be returned, the same after retaining copies of such document duly authenticated thereof.

(3) The provisions of the code of criminal procedure, 1973 relating to searches shall, so far as may be, apply to searches under this section subject to the modification that sub-section (5) of section 165 of the said code shall have effect as if for the words "magistrate", wherever it occurs therein, the words "Lokpal" or any officer authorized by it" were substituted.

17. Reports

(1) After the conclusion of inquiry, the Lokpal shall determine whether all or nay of the offences alleged in the memorandum of complaints have or has been prove to its

satisfaction and by report in writing shall communicate its findings to the complainant , the public functionary and the competent authority.

(2) The speaker, in the case of the Prime Minister or a Member of the of the people, and the chairman of the council of the states in the case of member of that council shall, as soon as may be, after the receipt of report under sub-section (1), cause the same to be laid before the House of the People of the Council of States, as the case may be while it is in session, and if the House of the people or the Council of states as the case may be, is not in session, within a period of one week from the reassembly of the said House or the Council, as the case may be.

(3) The competent authority shall examine the report forwarded to it under sub-section (1) and communicate to the Lokpal, with in a period of ninety days from the date of receipt of the report, the action taken or proposed to be taken on the basis of the report.

(4) The Lokpal shall present annually to the president a consolidated report on the administration of this act and the president shall, as soon as may be after and in any case not later than ninety days from the receipt of such report, cause the same , together with an explanatory memorandum, to be laid before Each House of Parliament.

Explanation: In computing the period of ninety days referred to in this sub-section, any period during which parliament or, is not in session, shall be excluded.

CHAPTER - IV : MISCELLANEOUS

18. Expenditure on chairperson and members to be charged on the consolidated fund of India. The salaries, allowances and pension payable to, or respect of, the Chairperson and Members of the Lokpal, shall be expenditure charged on the Consolidated Fund of India.

19. Intentional insult or Interruption to Lokpal

(1) Whoever intentionally offers any insult, or causes any interruption , to the Lokpal while the Lokpal or any of its

Members is making any verification or conducting any inquiry under this Act, shall be punished with simple imprisonment for term which may extend to six months , or fine . or with

(2) The provisions of sub-section (2) of section 199 of the code of Criminal procedure 1973, shall apply in relation to an offence referred to in sub-section (2) of the said section, subject to the modification that no memorandum of complaints in respect of such offence shall be made by the public Prosecutor except with the previous sanction of the lokpal.

20. Power of Lokpal try certain offences

(1) When any such offence as described in sub-section (1) of section 19 is committed in the view or presence of the Lokpal the Lokpal may cause the offender to be detained in custody and may at any time on the same day take cognizance of the offence and after giving the offender a reasonable opportunity of showing cause why he should not be punished under this section, try such offender summarily , so far as may be, in accordance with the procedure specified for a term which may extend to one month, or with fine which may extend to five hundred rupees, or with both.

(2) In every case tried under this section, the Lokpal shall record the facts constituting the offence with the statement, if any made by the offender as well as the fining and the sentence.

(3) Any person convicted on a trial held under this section may appeal to the supreme Court.

(4) The Provisions of this section shall have effect notwithstanding anything contained in the Code of Criminal Procedure 1973.

21. Disposal of deposit under section 12 etc., and penalty for malafide memorandum oc complaints.

(1) The sum deposited by a complainant in Pursuance of the provision of section 12 shall—

- In a case where the memorandum of complaints dismissed under sub-section (1) of section 13, stand forfeited to the Central Government

- If the Lokpal for reasons to be recorded in writing so directs, be utilized for compensating the public functionary comp lamed against, and
- In any other case be refunded to the complainant.

(2) If the Lokpal is satisfied that

- all or any of the allegation made in a memorandum of complainant have or has been substantiated either wholly or partly; and
- having regard to the expenses incurred by the complainant in reaction to the proceeding in react of such memorandum of complaints and all other relevant circumstances of the case the complainant deserves to be compensated or rewarded, the Lokpal shall determine the amount which shall be paid to the complainant by way of such compensation or reward and the lokpal shall determine the person by whom the said compensation or reward shall be paid after giving that person a reasonable opportunity of being heard.

(3) Every person who makes any memorandum of complaints which is held by the lokpal to be false and filed with malafide intention to harass the public functionary against whom such memorandum of complaints is filed shall be punishable as provided in Sub-section (4).

(4) When any offence under sub-section (3) is committed the lokpal may take cognizance of the offence and after giving the offender a reasonable opportunity of snowing cause why he should not be punished for such offence try such offender summarily so for as may be in accordance with the procedure specified for summary that's under the code of criminal Procedure, 1973 and if such offender is found guilty of committing the offence sentence him to imprisonment for a term which shall not be less than one year but which may extend to tree year and also to fine which may extend to fifty thousand rupees and may also award where fine to the public functionary against whom such false memorandum of complaints has been made such amount of compensation as the lokpal thinks fit.

22. Application of Act 2 of 1974. Notwithstanding anything contained in the Code of Criminal procedure 197 and subject to the other provisions of this act any case pending before the Lokpal under sub-section (4) of section 21 shall any be transferred to another criminal court in accordance with the procedure contained in section 407 of that code and for the purposes of that section the lokpal shall be deemed tó a court of session.

23. Conferment of additional function on Lokpal.

(1) The president may, by order in writing and subject to sub condition or limitations as may be specified in the order , require the Lokpal to inquire into any allegation (being an allegation in respect of which a memorandum of complaints may be made) specified in the provisions of section 13 the lokpal shall comply whit such order.

(2) When the Lokpal is to make any inquiry under sub- section (1) the Lokpal N shall exercise the same powers and discharge the same functions as would in the case of any inquiry made on a memorandum of complaints under this act and the provisions of this act except section 21 shall apply accordingly

24. Person likely to be prejudicially affected to be heard. If any stage of the inquiry , the Lokpal

(a) considerers it necessary to inquire into the conduct of any person: or

(b) is of opinion that the reputation of any person is likely to be prejudicially affected by the inquiry ;

The Lokpal shall give to the person a reasonable opportunity of being in the inquire and to Produce evidence in his deface'

Provided that nothing in this section shall apply where the credit of a withes is being impeached.

25. Protection of action taken in good faith.

(1) No suit prosecution or òther legal proceedings shall lie against the Lokpal or against any officer employee agency or person referred to in section 9, in respect of anything which is in good faith done or Intended to be done under this Act.

(2) Save as otherwise provided in this act on proceedings or decision of the Lokpal shall be called in question in any court.

26. Power to delegate. The Lokpal may by general or special order in writing and subject to such conditions and limitations in may be specified therein direct that any limitations as or duties imposed on it by or under this act {except the power under sub-section (1) of 12 the power to dismiss a memorandum of complaints under sub-section (1) of section 13 and the power under section21} may also be exercised or discharged by the officers employees and agencies referred to in section 9, as be specified in the order.

27. Power to make rules.

(1) The President may, by notification in the Official Gazette, make rules for the purpose of carrying out the provisions of this Act.

(2) In particular, and without prejudice to the generality of the foregoing power, such rules may provide for—

(a) the manner in which the President shall obtain the opinion of teh Chief Justice of India under sub-section (1) of setion 11;

(b) the form of memorandum of complaints under sub-section (2) of section 12 and the fess, if any, to be accompanied therewith;

(c) the manner in which and the authorities of agencies with whom deposit shall be made under sub-section (3)of section 12 and the form in which certificate shall be furnished in respect of such deposits;

(d) the matters referred to in sub-clause (vi) of clause (b)of sub-section (1) of section 15; and

(e) any other matter which is to be or may be prescribed;

(3) Every rule made under this Act shall be laid as soon as may be after it is made before each house of parliament while it is in session for a total period of thirty days while may be comprised in one sessions or in two or more successive session and if before the expiry of the session immediately following the sessions or the successive sessions aforesaid both houses agree in making any modification in the rule or

both houses agree that the rule should not be made the rule shall thereafter have affected only in such modified form or be of no effect as the case may be so however that any such modification or annulment shall be without prejudice to the validity of anything previous done under that rule.

28. Removal of doubts. For the removal of doubts it is hereby declared that nothing in this Act shall operate to confer or enable the conferring of any jurisdiction on the Lokpal to make any inquiry—

(a) into any allegation of corruption against or any act or conduct of—

- the president the vice -president the speaker of the House of the People the Deputy Speaker of the House of the People Deputy Chairman of the Council of States;
- the Chief Justice or any other judge of the High Court or the Supreme Court;
- the comptroller and Attorney General of India Chairman and other member of National Commission for Scheduled Castes and Scheduled tribes, teh Chief Eclection Commissioner other Election Commissioner, the Chairman and other Members of the Union Public Service Commission or nay other authority appointed under the Constitution of India; and

(b) upon its own knowledge or information.

29. Savings. Nothing contained in this Act shall be construed as affecting the consititution of, or the continuance of, functioning or exercise of powers by any Commission of Inquiry appointed under the Commissions of Inquiry Act, 1952 before the commencement of this act and no memorandum of complaints shall be made under this Act in respect of any matter referred for inquiry to such Commission before such commencement.

30. Amendment of Act 60 of 1952. In secction 3 of the Commisions of Inquiry Act, 1952, in sub-section (1), for the words "The appropriate Government may", the word, brackets and figures "Subject to the provisions of sub-section (3) of section (3) of section 10 of the Lockpal Act, 2007, the appropriate Government may" shall be substituted.

THE SCHEDULE
[See section 3(3)]

I, A.B .... having been appointed Chairperson for a Member) of the Lokpal co swear in the name of God/solemnly affirm that I will bear true faith and allegiance to teh Constitution of India as by law established, that I will duly and faithfully and to the best of my ability, knowledge and judgement perform the duties of my office without fear or favour, affection or ill-will.

❑❑❑

7

Jan Lokpal Bill by Public

An act to create effective anti-corruption and grievance redressal systems at centre so that effective deterrent is created against corruption and to provide effective protection to whistleblowers.

1. Short title and commencement.

(1) This Act may be called the Anti-Corruption, Grievance Redressal And Whistleblower Protection Act, 2010.

(2) It shall come into force on the one hundred and twentieth day of its enactment.

2. Definitions. In this Act, unless the context otherwise requires,-

(1) "Action" means any action taken by a public servant in the discharge of his functions as such public servant and includes decision, recommendation or finding or in any other manner and includes willful failure or omission to act and all other expressions relating to such action shall be construed accordingly;

(2) "Allegation" in relation to a public servant includes any affirmation that such public servant—

(a) has indulged in misconduct, if he is a government servant;

(b) has indulged in corruption

(3) "complaint" includes any grievance or allegation or a request by whistleblower for protection and appropriate action.

(4) "corruption" includes anything made punishable under Chapter IX of the Indian Penal Code or under the Prevention of Corruption Act, 1988;

Provided that if any person obtains any benefit from the government by violating any laws or rules, that person along with the public servants who directly or indirectly helped that person obtain those benefits. shall be deemed to have indulged in corruption.

(5) "Government" or "Central Government" means Government of India.

(6) "Government Servant" means any person who is or was any time appointed to a civil service or post in connection with the affairs of the Central Government or High Courts or Supreme Court either on deputation or permanent or temporary or on contractual employment but would not include the judges.

(7) "grievance" means a claim by a person that he sustained injustice or undue hardship in consequence of mal-administration;

(8) "Lokpal" means—

a. Benches constituted under this Act and performing their functions as laid down under various provisions of this Act; or

b. Any officer or employee, exercising its powers and carrying out its functions and responsibilities, in the manner and to the extent, assigned to it under this Act, or under various rules, regulations or orders made under various provisions of this Act.

c. For all other purposes, the Chairperson and members acting collectively as a body;

(9) "Mal-administration" means action taken or purporting to have been taken in the exercise of administrative function in any case where,

a. such action or the administrative procedure or practice governing such action is unreasonable, unjust, oppressive or improperly discriminatory; or

b. there has been willful negligence or undue delay in taking such action or the administrative procedure or practice governing such action involves undue delay;

(10) "Misconduct" means misconduct as defined in CCS Conduct Rules and which has vigilance angle. (11)"public authority" means any authority or body or institution of self- government established or constituted—

a. by or under the Constitution;

b. by any other law made by Parliament;

c. by notification issued or order made by the Government, and includes any body owned, controlled or substantially financed by the Government;

(12) "Public servant" means a person who is or was at any time,-

(a) the Prime Minister;

(b) a Minister;

(c) a Member of Parliament;

(d) Judges of High Courts and Supreme Court;

(e) a Government servant;

(f) the Chairman or Vice-Chairman (by whatever name called) or a member of a local authority in the control of the Central Government or a statutory body or corporation established by or under any law of the Parliament of India, including a co-operative society, or a Government Company within the meaning of section 617 of the Companies Act, 1956 and members of any Committee or Board, statutory or non- statutory, constituted by the Government;

(g) Such other authorities as the Central Government may, by notification, from time to time, specify;
(13)"Vigilance angle" includes -

(a) All acts of corruption

(b) Gross or willful negligence; recklessness in decision making; blatant violations of systems and procedures; exercise of discretion in excess, where no ostensible/ public interest is evident; failure to keep the controlling authority/superiors informed in time

(c) Failure/delay in taking action, if under law the government servant ought to do so, against subordinates on complaints of corruption or dereliction of duties or abuse of office by the subordinates

(d) Indulging in discrimination through one's conduct, directly or indirectly.

(e) Victimizing Whistle Blowers

(f) Any undue/unjustified delay in the disposal of a case, perceived after considering all relevant factors, would reinforce a conclusion as to the presence of vigilance angle in a case.

(g) Make unfair investigation or enquiry to either unduly help culprits or fabricate the innocent. (h) Any other matter as notified from time to time by Lokpal

(14) "Whistleblower" is any person who faces threat of (1) professional harm, including but not limited to illegitimate transfers, denial of promotions, denial of appropriate perks, departmental proceedings, discrimination or (2) physical harm or (3) is actually subjected to such harm; because of either making a complaint to Lokpal under this Act or for filing an application under Right to Information Act.

3. Establishment of the institution of Lokpal and appointment of Lokpal.

(1) There shall be an institution known as Lokpal which shall consist of one Chairperson and ten members along with its officers and employees. The Lokpal shall be headed by its Chairperson.

(2) The Chairperson and members of Lokpal shall be selected in such manner as laid down in this Act.

(3) A person appointed as Chairperson or member of Lokpal shall, before entering upon his office, make and subscribe before the President, an oath or affirmation in the form as prescribed.

(4) The Government shall appoint the Chairperson and members of the first Lokpal and set up the institution with all its logistics and assets within six months of enactment of this Act.

(5) The Government shall fill up a vacancy of the Chairperson or a member caused due to: a) Retirement, 3 months before the member or the Chairperson retires. b) Any other unforeseen reason, within a month of such vacancy..

CHAIRPERSON AND MEMBERS OF LOKPAL

4. The Chairperson and members of Lokpal not to have held certain offices. The Chairperson and members of Lokpal shall not be serving or former member of either the Parliament or the Legislature of any State and shall not hold any office or trust of profit (other than the office as Chairperson or member) or would have ever been connected with any political party or carry on any business or practice any profession and accordingly, before he enters upon his office, a person appointed as the Chairperson or member of Lokpal shall-

(i) if he holds any office of trust or profit, resign from such office; or

(ii) if he is carrying on any business, sever his connection with the conduct and management of such business; or

(iii) if he is practicing any profession, suspend practice of such profession.

(iv) If he is associated directly or indirectly with any other activity, which is likely cause conflict of interest in the performance of his duties in Lokpal, he should suspend his association with that activity.

Provided that if even after the suspension, the earlier association of that person with such activity is likely to adversely affect his performance at Lokpal, that person shall not be appointed as a member or Chairperson of Lokpal.

5. Term of office and other conditions of service of Lokpal.

(1) A person appointed as the Chairperson or member of Lokpal shall hold office for a term of five years from the date on which he enters upon his office;

Provided further that.-

(a) The Chairperson or member of Lokpal may, by writing under his hand addressed to the President, resign his office;

(b) The Chairperson or member may be removed from office in the manner provided in this Act.

(2) There shall be paid to the Chairperson and each member every month a salary equal to that of the Chief Justice of India and that of the judge of the Supreme Court respectively;

(3) The allowances and pension payable to and other conditions of service of the Chairperson or a member shall be such as may be prescribed;

Provided that the allowances and pension payable to and other conditions of service of the Chairperson or members shall not be varied to his disadvantage after his appointment.

(4) The administrative expenses of the office of the Lokpal including all salaries, allowances and pensions payable to or in respect of persons serving in that office, shall be charged on the Consolidated Fund of India.

(5) There shall be a separate fund by the name of "Lokpal fund" in which penalties/fines imposed by the Lokpal shall be deposited and in which 10% of the loss of Public Money detected/prevented on account of investigations by Lokpal shall also be deposited by the Government. Disposal of such fund shall be completely at the discretion of the Lokpal and such fund shall be used only for enhancement/upgradation/extension of the infrastructure of Lokpal.

(6) The Chairperson or members shall not be eligible for appointment on any position in Government of India or Government of any state or for fighting elections, if he has ever held the position of the Chairperson or a member for any period.

Provided however that a member or Chairperson may be reappointed for one more term or a member may be appointed as the Chairperson, however, that any person shall not serve for more than a total of two terms.

6. Appointment of the Chairperson and members.

1. The Chairperson and members shall be appointed by the President on the recommendation of a selection committee.
2. Following persons shall not be eligible to become Chairman or Member in Lokpal:
   (a) Any person who was ever chargesheeted for any offence under IPC or PC Act or was ever penalized under CCS Conduct Rules.
   (b) Any person who is less than 40 years in age.
3. At least four members of Lokpal shall have legal background.
4. The members and Chairperson should have unimpeachable integrity and should have demonstrated their resolve and efforts to fight against corruption in the past.
5. A selection committee consisting of the following shall be set up:

a. The Chairpersons of both Houses of Parliament
b. Two senior most judges of Supreme Court
c. Two senior most Chief Justices of High Courts.
d. All Nobel Laureates of Indian Origin
e. Chairperson of National Human Rights Commission
f. Last two Magsaysay Award winners of Indian origin
g. Comptroller and Auditor General of India
h. Chief Election Commissioner
i. Bharat Ratna Award winners
j. After the first set of selection process, the outgoing members and Chairperson of Lokpal.

6. The senior most judge of Supreme Court shall act as the Chairperson of the selection committee.
7. The following selection process shall be followed:
    a. Recommendations shall be invited through open advertisements in prescribed format.
    b. Each person recommending shall be expected to justify the selection of his candidate giving examples from the past achievements of the candidate.
    c. The list of candidates along with their recommendations received in the format mentioned above shall be displayed on a website.
    d. Each member of the selection committee, on the basis of the above material, shall recommend such number of names as there are vacancies
    e. A priority list shall be prepared with the candidate receiving recommendations from maximum number of members of selection committee at the top. The candidates recommended by same number of members shall be treated at par.
    f. This priority list shall be displayed on the website.
    g. Around three times the names as there are vacancies, shall be shortlisted from the top.

h. Public feedback shall be invited on the shortlisted names by putting these names on the website.

i. The selection committee may decide to use any means to collect more information about the background and past achievements of the shortlisted candidates.

j. Selection committee shall invite shortlisted candidates for discussions, video recordings of which shall be made public.

k. All the material obtained so far about the candidates shall be made available to each member of the selection committee in advance. The members shall make their own assessment of each candidate.

l. The selection committee shall meet and discuss the material so received about each candidate. The final selections for the Chairperson and members shall be made preferably through consensus.

   Provided that if three or more members, for reasons to be recorded in writing, object to the selection of any member, he shall not be selected.

m. All meetings of selection committee shall be video recorded and shall be made public.

8. The Prime Minister shall recommend the names finalized by the selection committee to the President immediately, who shall order such appointments within a month of receipt of the same.

9. If any of the members of the selection committee retires while a selection process is going on, that member will continue on the selection committee till the end of that process.

7. Removal of Chairperson or members.

(1) The Chairperson or any member shall not be removed from his office except by an order of the President.

(2) They can be removed on one or more of the following grounds:

a. Proved misbehavior

b. Professional or physical incapacity

c. If he is adjudged to be insolvent

d. Has been charged of an offence which involves moral turpitude

e. If he engages during his term of office in any paid employment outside the duties of his office

f. Has acquired such financial interests or other interests which are likely to affect prejudicially his functions as member or Chairperson.

g. If he is guided by considerations extraneous to the merits of the case either to favor someone or to implicate someone through any act of omission or commission.

h. If any member or Chairperson tries to or actually unduly influences any government functionary.

i. If he commits any act of omission or commission which is punishable under Prevention of Corruption Act or is a misconduct.

j. If a member or the Chairperson in any way, concerned or interested in any contract or agreement made by or on behalf of the Government of India or participates in any way in the profit thereof or in any benefit or emolument arising there from otherwise than as a member and in common with the other members of an incorporated company, he shall be deemed to be guilty of misbehavior.

(3) The following process shall be followed for the removal of any member or Chairperson:

(a) Any person may move an application/petition before the Supreme Court seeking removal of one or more of the members of Chairperson of Lokpal alleging one or more of the grounds for removal and providing evidence for the same.

(b) Supreme Court will hear the matter by a bench of three or more Judges on receipt of such petition and may take one or more of the following steps:

(i) order an investigation to be done by a Special Investigation Team appointed by the Supreme Court if a prima facie case is made out and if the matter cannot be judged based on affidavits of the parties. The Special Investigation Team shall submit its report within three months.

(ii) Pending investigations under sub-clause (i) by Special Investigation Team, the Supreme Court may decide to order withdrawal of part or complete work from that member. (iii) dismiss the petition if no case is made out. (iv) if the grounds are proved, recommend to the President for removal of the said member or Chairperson (v) direct registration and investigation of cases with appropriate agencies if there is prima facie case of commission of an offence punishable under Prevention of Corruption Act.

(c) The three judge bench shall be constituted by a panel of five senior most judges of the Supreme Court.

Provided that if there are any proceedings going on against any judge in Lokpal, he shall not be a part of either the panel or the bench.

(d) The Supreme Court shall not dismiss such petitions in liminae.

(e) If the Supreme Court concludes that the petition has been made with mischievous or malafide motives, the Court may order imposition of fine or imprisonment upto one year against the complainant.

(f) On receipt of a recommendation from the Supreme Court under this section, the Prime Minister shall recommend it to the President immediately and the President shall order removal of said members within a month of receipt of the same.

POWERS AND FUNCTIONS OF LOKPAL

8. Functions of Lokpal.

(1) Lokpal shall be responsible for receiving:

(a) Complaints where there are allegations of such acts of omission or commission which are punishable under Prevention of Corruption Act

(b) Complaints where there are allegations of misconduct by a government servant

(c) Grievances

(d) Complaints from whistleblowers

(2) Lokpal, after getting such enquiries and investigations done as it deems fit, may take one or more of the following actions:

a. Close the case if prima facie, the complaint is not made out or

b. Initiate prosecution against public servants as well as those private entities which are party to the act

c. Order imposition of appropriate penalties under CCS Conduct Rules

Provided that if an officer is finally convicted under Prevention of Corruption Act, major penalty of dismissal shall be imposed on such government servant. d. Order cancellation or modification of a license or lease or permission or contract or agreement, which was the subject matter of investigation.

e. Blacklist the concerned firm or company or contractor or any other entity involved in that act of corruption.

f. Issue appropriate directions to appropriate authorities for redressal of grievance in such time and in such manner as is specified in the order.

g. Invoke its powers under this Act if its orders are not duly complied with and ensure due compliance of its orders.

h. Take necessary action to provide protection to a whistleblower as per various provisions of this Act.

(3) Suo moto initiate appropriate action under this Act if any case, of the nature mentioned in clauses (1), (2), (3) or (4), comes to the knowledge of the Lokpal from any source.

(4) Issue such directions, as are necessary, from time to time, to appropriate authorities so as to make such changes in their work practices, administration or other systems so as to reduce the scope and possibility for corruption, misconduct and public grievances.

(5) Lokpal shall be deemed to be "Disciplinary authority" or "appointing authority" for the purpose of imposing penalties under CCS Conduct Rules.

(6) Section 19 of Prevention of Corruption Act shall be deleted.

(7) Section 197 of CRPC shall not apply to any proceedings under this Act. All permissions, which need to be sought for initiating investigations or for initiating prosecutions under any Act shall be deemed to have been granted once Lokpal grants such permissions.

9. Issue of Search Warrant, etc.

(1) Where, in consequence of information in his possession, the Lokpal

(a) has reason to believe that any person –

(i) to whom a summon or notice under this Act, has, been or might be issued, will not or would not produce or cause to be produced any property, document or thing which will be necessary or useful for or relevant to any inquiry or other proceeding to be conducted by him;

(ii) is in possession of any money, bullion, jewellery or other valuable article or thing and such money, bullion, jewellery or other valuable article or thing represents either wholly or partly income or property which has not been disclosed to the authorities for the purpose of any law or rule in force which requires such disclosure to be made; or

(b) considers that the purposes of any inquiry or other proceedings to be conducted by him will be served by a general search or inspection. he may by a search warrant authorize any Police officer not below the rank of an Inspector of Police to conduct a search or carry out an inspection in accordance therewith and in particular to, -

(i) enter and search any building or place where he has reason to suspect that such property, document, money, bullion, jewellery or other valuable article or thing is kept;

(ii) search any person who is reasonably suspected of concealing about his person any article for which search should be made;

(iii) break open the lock of any door, box, locker safe, almirah or other receptacle for exercising the powers conferred by sub-clause (i) where the keys thereof are not available.

Seize any such property, document, money, bullion, jewellery or other valuable article or thing found as a result of such search;

(iv) place marks of identification on any property or document or make or cause to be made; extracts or copies there from; or

(v) make a note or an inventory of any such property, document, money, bullion, Jewellery or other valuable article or thing.

(2) The provisions of the Code of Criminal Procedure, 1973, relating to search and seizure shall apply, so far as may be, to searches and seizures under sub-section (1).

(3) A warrant issued under sub-section (1) shall for all purposes, be deemed to be a warrant issued by a court under section 93 of the Code of Criminal Procedure, 1973.

10. Evidence.

(1) Subject to the provisions of this section, for the purpose of any investigation (including the preliminary inquiry, if any, before such investigation) under this Act, the Lokpal may require any public servant or any other person who, in his opinion is able to furnish information or produce documents relevant to the investigation, to furnish any such information or produce any such document.

(2) For the purpose of any such investigation (including the preliminary inquiry) the Lokpal shall have all the powers of a civil court while trying a suit under the Code of Civil Procedure, 1908 , in respect of the following matters, namely:-

(a) Summoning and enforcing the attendance of any person and examining him on oath;

(b) Requiring the discovery and production of any document;

(c) Receiving evidence on affidavits;

(d) Requisitioning any public record or copy thereof from any court or office;

(e) Issuing commissions for the examination of witnesses or documents;

(f) Ordering payment of compensatory cost in respect of a false or vexatious claim or defence;

(g) ordering cost for causing delay;

(h) Such other matters as may be prescribed.

(3) Any proceeding before the Lokpal shall be deemed to be a judicial proceeding with in the meaning of section 193 of the Indian Penal Code.

11. Reports of Lokpal, etc.

(1) The Chairperson of Lokpal shall present annually a consolidated report in prescribed format on its performance to the President.

(2) On receipt of the annual report, the President shall cause a copy thereof together with an explanatory memorandum to be laid before each House of the Parliament.

(3) The Lokpal shall publish every month on its website the list of cases disposed with brief details of each such case, outcome and action taken or proposed to be taken in that case. It shall also publish lists of all cases received by the Lokpal during the previous month, cases disposed and cases which are pending.

12. Lokpal to be a deemed police officer.

(1) For the purposes of section 36 of Criminal Procedure Code, the Chairperson, members of Lokpal and the officers in investigation wing of Lokpal shall be deemed to be police officers.

(2) While investigating any offence under Prevention of Corruption Act 1988, they shall be competent to investigate any offence under any other law in the same case.

13. Powers in case of non-compliance of orders.

(1) Each order of Lokpal shall clearly specify the names of the officials who are required to execute that order, the manner in which it should be executed and the time period within which that order should be complied with.

(2) If the order is not complied with within the time or in the manner directed, Lokpal may decide to impose a fine on the officials responsible for the non-compliance of its orders.

(3) The Drawing and Disbursing Officer of that Department shall be directed to deduct such amount of fine as is clearly specified by the Lokpal in its order made in sub-section (2) from the salaries of the officers specified in the order.

Provided that no penalty shall be imposed without giving a reasonable opportunity of being heard.

Provided that if the Drawing and Disbursing Officer fails to deduct the salary as specified in the said order, he shall make himself liable for a similar penalty.

(4) In order to get its orders complied with, the Lokpal shall have, and exercise the same jurisdiction powers and authority in respect of contempt of itself as a High court has and may exercise, and, for this purpose, the provisions of the Contempt of Courts Act, 1971 (Central Act 70 of 1971) shall have the effect subject to the modification that the references therein to the High Court shall be construed as including a reference to the Lokpal.

13A. Special Judges under section 4 of Prevention of Corruption Act. On an annual basis, Lokpal shall make an assessment of the number of Special Judges required under section 4 of Prevention of Corruption Act 1988 in each area and the Government shall appoint such number of Judges within three months of receipt of such recommendation.

Provided that Lokpal shall recommend such number of Special Judges so that trial in each case under this Act is completed within a year.

13B. Issue of Letter Rogatory. A bench of Lokpal shall have powers to issue Letters Rogatory in any case pending with Lokpal.

FUNCTIONING OF LOKPAL

14. Functioning of Lokpal.

(1) The Chairperson shall be responsible for overall administration and supervision of the institution of Lokpal.

(2) All policy level decisions including formulation of regulations, developing internal systems for the functioning of Lokpal, assigning functions to various officials in Lokpal, delegation of powers to various functionaries in Lokpal etc shall be taken by the Chairperson and the members collectively as a body.

(3) The Chairperson shall have an annual meeting with the Prime Minister to assess the needs of Lokpal for finances and manpower. Lokpal shall be provided resources by the Government on the basis of outcome of this meeting.

(4) Lokpal shall function in benches of three or more members. Benches shall be constituted randomly and cases shall be assigned to them randomly by computer. Each bench shall consist of at least one member with legal background.

(5) Such benches shall be responsible for

(i) granting permission to close any case after a preliminary enquiry

(ii) granting permission to either close a case after investigations or issuing orders imposing penalties under CCS Conduct Rules and/or for initiating prosecution in that case.

(iii) Issuing orders under section 28 and section 13B.

(6) Lokpal may decide to initiate investigations into any case suo moto also.

(7) The decision to initiate investigation or prosecution against any member of the Cabinet or any judge of High Court or Supreme Court shall be taken in a meeting of all the existing members and the Chairperson. Minutes and records of such meetings shall be made public.

15. Making a complaint to the Lokpal.

(1) Subject to the provisions of this Act, any person may make a complaint under this Act to the Lokpal.

Provided that in case of a grievance, if the person aggrieved is dead or for any reason, unable to act for himself, the complaint may be made or if it is already made may be continued by his legal representatives or by any other person who is authorized by him in writing in this behalf.

(2) A complaint could be on a plain paper but should contain all such details as prescribed by Lokpal.

(3) On receipt of a complaint, the Lokpal shall decide whether it is an allegation or a grievance or a request for whistleblower protection or a mixture of two or more of these.

(4) Every complaint shall have to be compulsorily disposed off by the Lokpal.

Provided that no complaint, other than those which are anonymous or pseudonymous, shall be closed without hearing the complainant.

16. Matters which may be investigated by the Lokpal. Subject to the provisions of this Act, the Lokpal may investigate any action which is taken by or with the general or specific approval of a public servant where a complaint involving a grievance or an allegation is made in respect of such action.

Provided that the Lokpal may also investigate such action suo moto or if it is referred to it by the government, if such action can be or could have been in his recorded opinion, subject of a grievance or an allegation.

17. Matters not subject to investigation.

(1) The Lokpal shall not conduct any investigation under this Act in case of a grievance in respect of any action-

(i) If the complainant has or had, any remedy by way of appeal, revision, review or any other remedy before any other authority provided in any other law and he has not availed of the same.

(ii) Taken by a judicial or quasi-judicial body, unless the complainant alleges malafides

(iii) If the substance of the entire grievance is pending before any court or quasi-judicial body of competent jurisdiction.

(iv) any grievance where there is inordinate and inexplicable delay.

(2) Nothing in this Act shall be construed as authorising the Lokpal to investigate any action which is taken by or with the approval of the Presiding Officer of either House of Parliament.

(3) The provisions of this Act shall be in addition to the provisions of any other enactment or any rule or law under which any remedy by way of appeal, revision, review or in any other manner is available to a person making a complaint under this Act in respect of any action and nothing in this Act shall limit or affect the right of such person to avail of such remedy.

(4) Nothing in this section shall bar Lokpal from entertaining a complaint making an allegation of misconduct or corruption or a complaint from a whistleblower seeking protection.

18. Provisions relating to complaints and investigations.

(i) (a) The Lokpal, on receipt of a complaint in the nature of an allegation or a grievance or a combination of the two, or in a case initiated on his own motion, may on perusing the documents, either decide to proceed to enquire or investigate into that complaint or decide, to make such preliminary inquiry before proceeding to enquire or investigate into such complaint or direct any other person to make such preliminary inquiry as it deems fit for ascertaining whether there exists reasonable ground for conducting the investigation. The outcome of such preliminary enquiry, and if the complaint is being closed along with reasons for the same and all material collected during preliminary enquiry, shall be communicated to the complainant.

Provided that if any case is closed, all documents related thereto shall thereafter be treated as public. Every month, a list of all such cases shall be put on the website with reasons for closing a case. All material connected with such closed cases will be provided to anyone seeking it under Right to Information Act.

Provided further that if the complaint contains verifiable and specific information about misconduct or corruption, then that case shall not be rejected even if the complaint is anonymous.

Provided further that no complaint of allegation shall be rejected by questioning the motives or intention of the complainant.

Provided further that all hearings before Lokpal shall be video recorded and shall be available to any member of the public on payment of copying costs.

(b) The procedure for preliminary enquiry of a complaint shall be such as the Lokpal deems appropriate in the circumstances of the case and in particular, the Lokpal may, if it deems necessary to do so, call for the comments of the public servant concerned.

Provided that the preliminary enquiry should be completed and a decision taken whether to close a case or to proceed with investigations within one month of receipt of any complaint.

(ii) Where the Lokpal proposes, either directly or after making preliminary inquiry, to conduct any investigation under this Act, he.-

(a) may make such order as to the safe custody of documents relevant to the investigation, as it deems fit.

(b) at appropriate stage of investigations or in the end, it shall forward a copy of the complaint, its findings and copy of the material relied upon to the concerned public servant and the complainant,

(c) shall afford to such public servant and the complainant an opportunity to offer comments and be heard.

Provided that such hearing shall be held in public, except in such rare circumstances, to be recorded in writing, will it be held in camera.

(iii) The conduct of an investigation under this Act against a Public servant in respect of any action shall not affect such action, or any power or duty of any other public servant to take further action with respect to any matter subject to the investigation.

(iv) If, during the course of preliminary inquiry or investigation under this Act, the Lokpal is prima facie satisfied that the allegation or grievance in respect of any action is likely to be sustained either wholly or partly, he may, through an interim order, direct the public servant concerned to stay the implementation or enforcement of the decision or action complained against, or to take such mandatory or preventive action, on such terms and conditions, as he may specify in his order to prevent further harm from taking place.

(v) The Lokpal, either during the course of investigations, if it is satisfied that prosecution is likely to be initiated in that case, or at the end of the investigations at the time of initiating prosecution, shall make a list of moveable and immoveable assets of all the accused in that case and shall notify the same. No transfer of the same shall be permitted after such notification. In the event of final conviction, the court shall be empowered to recover loss determined under section 19 of this Act from this property, in addition to other measures.

(vi) If during the course of investigation or enquiry into a complaint, Lokpal feels that continuance of a public servant in that position could adversely affect the course of investigations or enquiry or that the said person is likely to impact evidence or witnesses, the Lokpal may issue appropriate orders including transfer of that public servant from that position or his suspension.

Provided that such orders shall not be passed against the Prime Minister.

(vii) In case of a grievance, the Lokpal may issue interim orders to the appropriate authority recommending grant of interim relief to the complainant if he is satisfied at any stage of preliminary inquiry on investigation that the complainant has sustained injustice or undue hardship in consequence of any decision or action of a public servant.

(viii) The Lokpal may, at any stage of inquiry or investigation under this Act, direct through an interim order, appropriate authorities to take such action as is necessary, including suspension of a government servant, pending inquiry or investigation.-

(i) to safeguard wastage or damage of public property or public revenue by the administrative acts of the public servant;

(ii) to prevent further acts of misconduct by the public servant;

(iii) to prevent the public servant from secreting the assets allegedly acquired by him by corrupt means;

(ix) Where after investigation into a complaint, the Lokpal is satisfied that the complaint involving an allegation against the public servant is substantiated and that the public servant concerned should not continue to hold the post held by him, the Lokpal shall pass orders to that effect. In case of public servant being a Minister, Lokpal shall make such recommendation to the President, who shall decide either to accept such recommendation or reject it within a month of its receipt.

Provided that the provisions of this section shall not apply to the Prime Minister.

(x) If, after enquiry into a grievance and after affording reasonable opportunity of being heard to both the complainant and the public authority, the Lokpal is satisfied that such grievance is substantiated either wholly or partly, he shall,

i. Pass appropriate orders directing appropriate authorities to redress the grievance in a manner and within the time prescribed in the order, and

ii. Direct the appropriate authorities to deduct from the salary of the officials mentioned in the order, such penalty amounts as are directed by Lokpal, which shall not be less than Rs 250 per day of delay calculated from day the time limit mentioned in citizens' charter for redressing that grievance got over, and

iii. Direct the appropriate authorities to compensate the complainant with such amounts as mentioned in the order.

Provided that any grievance shall be disposed within 15 days of its receipt.

Provided further that if it relates to life and liberty of a person or if the matter is such as to warrant immediate attention and the Lokpal is so satisfied, the same shall be disposed within 48 hours.

(xi) All records and information of Lokpal shall be public and shall be provided under Right to Information Act, even at the stage of investigation or enquiry, unless release of such information would adversely affect the process of enquiry or investigation.

Provided that no information in any case shall be withheld under Right to Information Act after the completion of enquiry or investigation.

RECOVERY OF LOSS TO THE GOVERNMENT AND PUNISHMENTS

19. Recovery of loss to the Government. If a person is convicted of an offence under Prevention of Corruption Act, then the trial court will also quantify the loss caused to the government and apportion that amount to various convicts from whom this money must be recovered as arrears of land revenue.

19A. Punishments for offences. For offences mentioned in Chapter III of Prevention of Corruption Act, punishment shall not be less than five years which may extend upto life imprisonment.

Provided that if the accused is any officer of the rank of Joint Secretary in the state or above or a Minister, the punishment shall not be less than ten years.

Provided further that if the offence is of the nature mentioned in proviso to section 2(4) of this Act and if the beneficiary is any corporate house, in addition to other punishments mentioned in this Act and under Prevention of Corruption Act, a fine amounting to five times the loss caused to the government shall be recovered from the accused and the recovery may be done from the assets of the company and from the personal assets of all Directors of the company, if the assets of the accused are inadequate.

WHISTLEBLOWER PROTECTION

20. Protection of Whistleblower.

(1) A whistleblower may write to Lokpal seeking protection from threat of physical or professional victimization or if he has been subjected to such professional or physical victimization.

(2) On receiving such a complaint, Lokpal shall take following steps:

(a) Threat of professional victimization: Lokpal shall conduct appropriate enquiries and if it feels that there is a real threat to the person and the threat is on account of that person having made an allegation under this Act, then the Lokpal shall pass appropriate orders, as soon as possible but in not more than a month of receipt of such complaint, directing appropriate authorities to take such steps as directed by the Lokpal.

(b) If a person complains that he has already been victimized professionally on account of making an allegation under this Act, Lokpal shall, after conducting enquiries, if he is of the opinion that the victimization is indeed because of that person's having made an allegation under this

Act, pass appropriate orders, as soon as possible but in not more than a month, directing appropriate authorities to take such steps as directed by the Lokpal.

Provided that for clause (a) Lokpal may, but for clause (b) the Lokpal shall, also issue orders imposing penalties under CCS Conduct Rules against the officer or officials who issued threats or caused victimization.

Provided further that no such penalties shall be imposed without giving an opportunity of being heard to the affected officials.

(c) Threat of physical victimization: Lokpal shall conduct appropriate enquiries and if it feels that there is a real threat to the person and the threat is on account of that person having made an allegation under this Act or for having filed an RTI application to any public authority covered under this Act, then notwithstanding anything contained in any other law, the Lokpal shall pass appropriate orders, as soon as possible but in not more than a week, directing appropriate authorities, including police, to take such steps as directed by the Lokpal to provide adequate security to that person, to register criminal cases against those who are issuing threats and also to take all such steps necessary to mitigate circumstances leading to such threat.

Provided that if the threat is imminent, Lokpal may decide to act immediately, within a few hours to prevent physical assault on that person.

(d) If a person complains that he has already been physically assaulted on account of making an allegation under this Act and if Lokpal is satisfied after conducting enquiries that the person has been assaulted because of his having made an allegation under this Act or for filing an RTI application in any of the public authorities covered under this Act, then notwithstanding anything else contained in any other law, the Lokpal shall pass such orders, as soon as possible but in not more than 24 hours, directing the concerned authorities to take such steps as directed by the Lokpal to provide adequate security to that person, to register criminal cases and also to ensure that no further harm visits on that person.

(e) If the whistleblower has alleged an act punishable under Prevention of Corruption Act, then for cases under clause (c), Lokpal may and for cases under clause (d), the Lokpal shall, assign the allegations made by that person to a special team, put it on a fast track and complete investigations in that case in not more than a month.

(f) If the whistleblower has alleged an act punishable under any law other than the Prevention of Corruption Act, then for cases under clause (c), Lokpal may and for cases under clause (d), the Lokpal shall, direct the agency which has the powers to enforce that law to assign the allegations made by the whistleblower to a special team, put it on a fast track and complete investigations in that case in such time as directed by the Lokpal.

(g) Lokpal shall have the powers to issue directions to appropriate agencies in the cases covered under clause (f), monitor such investigations and if necessary, issue directions to that agency to do the investigations in the manner as directed by the Lokpal.

(3) If any complainant requests that his identity should be kept secret, Lokpal shall ensure the same. Lokpal shall prescribe detailed procedures on how such complainants shall be dealt with.

(4) Lokpal shall Issue orders to the Public Authorities to make necessary changes in their policies and practices to prevent recurrence of victimization.

GRIEVANCE REDRESSAL SYSTEMS

21. Citizens' Charters.

(1) Each public authority shall be responsible for ensuring the preparation and implementation of Citizens Charter, within a reasonable time, and not exceeding one year from the coming into force of this Act.

(2) Every Citizens Charter shall enumerate the commitments of the respective public authority to the citizens, officer responsible for meeting each such commitment and the time limit with in which the commitment shall be met.

(3) Each public authority shall designate an official called Public Grievance Redressal Officer, whom a complainant should approach for any violation of the Citizens Charter.

(4) Every public authority shall review and revise its Citizens Charter at least once every year through a process of public consultation.

(5) Lokpal may direct any public authority to make such changes in their citizens' charter as are mentioned in that order.

(6) No grievance shall be accepted by Lokpal if 15 days have not elapsed after submission of complaint by the complainant with the Public Grievance redressal Officer of that Public Authority.

Provided that if Lokpal feels that considering the gravity or urgency of the grievance, it is necessary to do so, the Lokpal may decide to accept such grievance earlier also.

EMPLOYEES AND STAFF AND AUTHORITIES IN LOKPAL

22. Chief Vigilance Officer.

(1) There shall be a Chief Vigilance Officer in each public authority to be selected and appointed by Lokpal.

(2) He shall not be from the same public authority.

(3) He shall be a person of impeccable integrity and ability to take proactive measures against corruption.

(4) He shall be responsible for accepting complaints against any public authority and shall transfer the complaints related to other public authorities within two days of receipt.

(5) He shall be responsible for carrying out all such responsibilities as assigned to him from time to time by Lokpal including dealing with complaints in the manner as laid down by Lokpal from time to time. Provided that the complaints which require investigations under Prevention of Corruption Act 1988 shall be transferred to the Investigative wing of Lokpal.

Provided further that the complaints, other than grievances, against officers of the level of Joint Secretary or above shall not be dealt by the Chief Vigilance Officer and shall be transferred to the Lokpal, who shall set up a committee of Chief Vigilance Officers of three other public authori.ies to enquire into such complaint.

(6) All the grievances shall be received and disposed by Chief Vigilance Officer on behalf of Lokpal, if the citizen fails to get satisfactory redressal from Public Grievance Officer under section 21 of this Act.

23. Staff of Lokpal, etc.

(1) There shall be such officers and employees as may be prescribed to assist the Lokpal in the discharge of their functions under this Act.

(2) The number and categories of officers and employees shall be decided by the Lokpal in consultation with the government.

(3) The categories, recruitment and conditions of service of the officers and employees referred in sub-section (1) including such special conditions or special pay as may be necessary for enabling them to act without fear in the discharge of their functions, shall be such as may be prescribed according to the recommendations of Lokpal.

Provided that no official, whose integrity is in doubt, shall be considered for being posted in Lokpal.

Provided further that all officers and employees, who work in Lokpal on deputation or otherwise shall be eligible for the same terms and conditions as prescribed under this clause.

(4) Without prejudice to the provisions of sub-section (1), the Lokpal may for the purpose of conducting investigations under this Act utilize the services of.-

- (a) any officer or investigating agency of the Central Government; or
- (b) any officer or investigating agency of any other Government with the prior concurrence of that Government; or
- (c) any person or any other agency.

(5) The officers and other employees referred to in sub-section (1) shall be under the administrative and disciplinary control of the Lokpal:

(6) Lokpal shall have the powers to choose its own officials. Lokpal may enlist officials on deputation from other government agencies for a fixed tenure or it may enlist officials on permanent basis from other government agencies or it may appoint people from outside on permanent basis or on a fixed tenure basis.

(7) The staff and officers shall be entitled to such pay scales and other allowances, which may be different

and more than the ordinary pay scales in the Central Government, as are decided by the Lokpal from time to time, in consultation with the Prime Minister, so as to attract honest and efficient people to work in Lokpal.

24. Repeal and savings.

(1) The Central Vigilance Commission Act shall stand repealed.

(2) Notwithstanding such repeal, any act or thing done under the said Act shall be deemed to have been done under this Act and may be continued and completed under the corresponding provisions of this Act.

(3) All enquiries and investigations and other disciplinary proceedings pending before the Central Vigilance Commission and which have not been disposed of, shall stand transferred to and be continued by the Lokpal as if they were commenced before him under this Act.

(4) Notwithstanding anything contained in any Act, the posts of the Secretary and other Officers and Employees of the Central Vigilance Commission are hereby abolished and they are hereby appointed as the Secretary and other officers and employees of the Lokpal. The salaries, allowances and other terms and conditions of services of the said Secretary, officers and other employees shall, until they are varied, be the same as to which they were entitled to immediately before the commencement of this Act.

(5) All vigilance administration under the control of all Departments of Central Government, Ministries of the Central Government, corporations established by or under any Central Act, Government companies, societies and local authorities owned or controlled by the Central Government shall stand transferred, along with its personnel, assets and liabilities to Lokpal for all purposes.

(6) The personnel working in vigilance wings of the agencies mentioned in sub-section (5) shall be deemed

to be on deputation to Lokpal for a period of five years from the date they are transferred to Lokpal. However, Lokpal may decide to repatriate any one of them anytime.

(7) That Department from where any personnel have been transferred to Lokpal under sub-section (5), shall cease to have any control over the administration and functions of transferred personnel.

(8) Lokpal shall rotate the personnel and create vigilance wing of each department in such a way that no personnel from the same department get posted for vigilance functions in the same department.

(9) No person shall be employed with Lokpal against whom any vigilance enquiry or any criminal case is pending at the time of being considered.

25. Investigation Wing of Lokpal.

(1) There shall be an investigation wing at Lokpal.

(2) Notwithstanding anything contained in section 17 of Prevention of Corruption Act, such officers of Investigation wing, upto the level as decided by Lokpal, shall have, in relation to the investigation and arrest of persons throughout India, in connection with investigation of complaints under this Act, all the powers, duties, privileges and liabilities which members of Delhi Special Police Establishment have in connection with the investigation of offences committed therein.

(3) That part of Delhi Special Police Establishment, in so far as it relates to investigation and prosecution of offences alleged to have been committed under the Prevention of Corruption Act, 1988, shall stand transferred, along with its employees, assets and liabilities to Lokpal for all purposes.

(4) That part of Delhi Special Police Establishment, which has been transferred under sub-section (3), shall form part of Investigation Wing of Lokpal.

(5) The Central Government shall cease to have any control over the transferred part and its personnel. (6) The salaries, allowances and other terms and conditions of services of the personnel transferred under sub-section (3) shall be the same as to which they were entitled to immediately before the commencement of this Act.

(7) All cases which were being dealt by that part of Delhi Special Police Establishment, which has been transferred under sub-section (3), shall stand transferred to Lokpal.

(8) After completion of investigation in any case, the investigation wing shall present the case to an appropriate bench of Lokpal, which shall decide whether to grant permission for prosecution or not.

26. Complaints against officers or employees of Lokpal.

(1) Complaints against employees or officers of Lokpal shall be dealt with separately and as per provisions of this section.

(2) Such complaint could relate to an allegation of an offence punishable under Prevention of Corruption Act or a misconduct or a dishonest enquiry or investigation.

(3) As soon as such a complaint is received, the same shall be displayed on the website of Lokpal, along with the contents of the complaint.

(4) Investigations into each such complaint shall be completed within a month of its receipt.

(5) In addition to examining the allegations against the said official, the allegations shall especially be examined against sections 107, 166, 167, 177, 182, 191, 192, 196, 199, 200, 201, 202, 204, 217, 218, 219, 463, 464, 468, 469, 470, 471, 474 of Indian Penal Code.

(6) If, during the course of investigations, the Lokpal feels that the charges are likely to be sustained, the Lokpal shall divest such officer of all his responsibilities and powers and shall place him under suspension.

(7) If after completion of enquiry or investigations, Lokpal decides to prosecute that person under Prevention of Corruption Act, 1988 or holds him guilty of any misconduct or of conducting dishonest enquiry or investigations, then that person shall not work with Lokpal anymore. Lokpal shall either dismiss that person from the job, if that person is in the employment of Lokpal, or shall repatriate him, if he is on deputation.

Provided that no order under this clause shall be passed without giving reasonable opportunity of being heard to the accused person.

Provided further that order under this clause shall be passed within 15 days of completion of investigations.

(8) There shall be a separate wing in Lokpal to deal with complaints against officers or staff of Lokpal. (9) Lokpal shall take all steps to ensure that all enquiries and investigations on complaints against its own staff and officials are conducted in most transparent and honest manner.

27. Protection.

(1) No suit, prosecution, or other legal proceedings shall lie against the Chairperson or members or against any officer, employee, agency or person referred to in Section 14(4) in respect of anything which is in good faith done while acting or purporting to act in the discharge of his official duties under this Act.

(2) No proceedings of the Lokpal shall be held to be bad for want of form and except on the ground of jurisdiction, no proceedings or decision of the Lokpal shall be liable to be challenged, reviewed, quashed or called in question in any court of ordinary Civil Jurisdiction.

MISCELLANEOUS

28. Public Servants to submit property statements.

(1) Every public servant, other than those mentioned in Section 2(11)(a) to (c), shall within three months after

the commencement of this Act and thereafter before the 30th June of every year submit to the head of that public authority, in the form prescribed by Lokpal, a statement of his assets and liabilities and those of the members of his family. Public servants mentioned in sections 2(11)(a) to (c) shall submit their returns in a format prescribed by the Lokpal to the Lokpal with the aforesaid time lines.

(2) The Head of each public authority shall ensure that all such statements are put on the website by 31st August of that year.

(3) If no such statement is received by the Head of that public authority from any such public servant within the time specified in sub-section (1), the Head of that public authority shall direct the concerned public servant to do so immediately. If within next one month, the public servant concerned does not submit such statement, the Head shall stop the salary and allowances of that public servant till he submits such statement.

Explanation: In this section "family of a public servant" means the spouse and such children and parents of the public servant as are dependent on him.

(4) The Lokpal may initiate prosecution against such public servant under Section 176 IPC.

(5) If any public servant furnishes any statement, which is subsequently found to be incorrect, then Lokpal, in addition to taking action against the said public servant under other sections of this Act, may also impose a penalty upto a maximum of 50% of the value of the additional property subsequently detected. Lokpal shall also intimate such information to the Income Tax Department for appropriate action.

29. Power to delegate and assign functions.

(1) Lokpal shall be competent to delegate its powers and assign functions to the officials working in Lokpal.

(2) All functions carried out and powers exercised by such officials shall be deemed to have been so done by the Lokpal.

Provided that the following functions shall be performed by the benches and cannot be delegated: (i) Granting permission to initiate prosecution in any case. (ii) Order for dismissal of any government servant under CCS Conduct Rules. (iii) Passing orders under section 10 on complaints against officials and staff of Lokpal. (iv) Pass orders in cases of complaints, other than grievances, against officers of the level of Joint Secretary and above.

30. Time limits.

(1) Preliminary enquiry under sub-section (1) of section 9 of this Act should be completed within a month of receipt of complaint.

Provided that the enquiry officer shall be liable for an explanation if the enquiry is not completed within this time limit.

(2) Investigation into any allegation shall be completed within six months, and in any case, not more than one year, from the date of receipt of complaint.

(3) Trial in any case filed by Lokpal should be completed within one year. Adjournments should be granted in rarest circumstances.

31. Penalty for false complaint.

(1) Notwithstanding anything contained in this Act, if someone makes any false or frivolous complaint under this Act, Lokpal may impose such fines on that complainant as it deems fit.

Provided that no fine can be imposed without giving a reasonable opportunity of being heard.

(2) Such fines shall be recoverable as dues under Land Revenue Act.

(3) A complaint or allegation once made under this Act shall not be allowed to be withdrawn.

31A. Preventive measures.

(1) Lokpal shall, at regular intervals, either study itself or cause to be studied the functioning of all public authorities falling within its jurisdiction and in consultation with respective public authority, issue such directions as it deems fit to prevent incidence of corruption in future.

(2) Lokpal shall also be responsible for creating awareness about this Act and involving general public in curbing corruption and maladministration.

32. Power to make Rules.

(1) The Government may, by notification in the Official Gazette, make rules for the purpose of carrying into effect the provisions of this Act.

Provided that such rules shall be made only in consultation and with the approval of Lokpal.

(2) In particular, and without prejudice to the generality of the foregoing provisions, such rules may provide for-

(i) the allowance and pensions payable to and other conditions of service of the Chairperson and members of Lokpal;

(ii) the powers of a Civil Court which may be exercised by the Lokpal under clause (h) of sub-section (2) of section 11;

(iii) the salary, allowances, recruitment and other conditions of service of the staff and employees of the Lokpal;

(iv) any other matter for which rules have to be made are necessary under this Act.

(3) Any rule made under this Act may be made with retrospective effect and when such a rule is made the reasons for making the rule shall be specified in a Statement laid before both Houses of the Parliament.

33. Removal of difficulties. Notwithstanding anything contained in this Act, the President, in consultation with Lokpal or on request of Lokpal may, by order, make such provision -

(i) for bringing the provisions of this Act into effective operation;

(ii) for continuing the enquiries and investigations pending before the Central Vigilance Commission by the Lokpal.

34. Power to make regulations. Lokpal shall have power to make its own regulations for the smooth functioning of the institution and to effectively implement various provisions of this Act.

35. This Act shall override the provisions of all other laws.

❑❑❑

Bibliography

Adas, Michael. *Machines as the Measure of Men: Science, Technology, and Ideologies of Western Dominance.* Ithaca: Cornell University Press, 1989.

Aggarwal, J.C. *National Policy on Education: Agenda for India 2001.* New Delhi: Concept, 1989.

Baker, Christopher J. *An Indian Rural Economy: The Tamiland Countryside.* Oxford: Clarendon Press, 1984.

Baxi, Upendra, and Bhikhu Parekh, eds. *Crisis and Change in Contemporary India.* New Delhi: Sage, in association with The Book Review Literary Trust, New Delhi, 1995.

Carras, Mary C. *Indira Gandhi in the Crucible of Leadership.* Boston: Beacon Press, 1979.

Central Board for the Prevention and Control of Water Pollution. *River Basin Atlas of India.* Calcutta: Center for Study of Man and Environment, Department of Geology, President College, 1985.

Damodaran, A.K., and Bajpai, U.S., eds. *Indian Foreign Policy: The Indira Gandhi Years.* New Delhi: Radiant, 1990.

Dynamics of Rural Development: Lessons From ralegan Siddhi Publisher- Foundation for Research in Community Health, 2002. Original from the University of Michigan.

Eaton, Richard M. *The Rise of Islam and the Bengal Frontier, 1204-1760.* Comparative Studies on Muslim Societies, No. 17. Berkeley: University of California Press, 1993.

Fairservis, Walter A. *The Roots of Ancient India: The Archaeology of Early Indian Civilization*. New York: Macmillan, 1971.

From Poverty to Plenty: The Story of Ralegan Siddhi Volume 5 of Studies in ecology and sustainable development. Authors- Ganesh Pangare, Vasudha Pangare. Publisher: Indian National Trust for Art and Cultural Heritage,1992. Original from the University of Virginia.

Gandhi, Mahatma. *An Autobiography: The Story of My Experiments with Truth*. Trans., Mahadev Desai. Boston: Beacon Press, 1957. Reprint. Boston: Beacon Press, 1993.

Habib, Irfan. *The Agrarian System of Mughal India, 1556-1707*. New York: Asia, 1963.

Inder Singh, Anita. "Decolonization in India: The Statement of February 20, 1947," *International History Review* [Toronto], 6, No. 2, May 1984, 191-209.

Ismail Serageldin, David R. Steeds (1998). *Rural well-being from vision to action*. World Bank Publications. pp. 433.

Jain, C.K., ed. *Rajiv Gandhi and Parliament*. New Delhi: CBS, 1992.

Kandaswamy, S.N. *Buddhism as Expounded in Manimekalai (The Jewelled Belt)*. Annamalainagar: Annamalai University, 1978.

Lelyveld, David. *Aligarh's First Generation*. Princeton: Princeton University Press, 1977.

Mahajan, Jagmohan. *The Raj Landscape: British Views of Indian Cities*. New Delhi: Spantech, 1988.

Mukhia, Harbans. *Perspectives on Medieval History*. New Delhi: Vikas, 1993.

Nanda, B.R. *The Indo-Greeks*. Oxford: Clarendon Press, 1957.

Nugent, Nicholas. *Rajiv Gandhi: Son of a Dynasty*. New Delhi: UBS, 1991.

Page, David. *Prelude to Partition: The Indian Muslims and the Imperial System of Control, 1920-1932*. Delhi: Oxford University Press, 1982.

Periwinkle Environmental Education Part-X Author-Harendra Chakhaiyar, Publisher- Jeevandeep Prakashan Pvt Ltd.

Qureshi, I.H. *The Muslim Community of the Indo-Pakistan Subcontinent, 1610-1947*. The Hague: Mouton, 1962.

Ralegan Siddhi Authors: Ramesh Awasthi, Dashrath K. Panmand, Foundation for Research in Community Health (Bombay, India) Publisher: Foundation for Research in Community Health, 1994. Original from The University of Michigan

Ramusack, Barbara N. *The Princes of India in the Twilight of Empire: Dissolution of a Patron-Client System, 1914-1939*. Columbus: Ohio State University Press, 1978.

Reilly, Carmel (2007). *Ralegan Siddhi: a special community*. Thomson Nelson. pp. 24 pages.

Religion and ecology in India and Southeast Asia Authors- David L. Gosling, Ninian Smart, Contributor- Ninian Smart, Edition- illustrated, Publisher- Routledge, 2001,

Sahasrabuddhe, P.G., and Manik Chandra Vajpayee. *The People Versus Emergency: A Saga of Struggle*. Trans., Sudhakar Raje. New Delhi: Suruchi Prakashan, 1991.

Seabrook, Jeremy (1993). *Victims of development: resistance and alternatives*. Verso. pp. 250.

Springs of life: India's water resources Authors Ganesh Pangare, Vasudha Pangare, Binayak Das, World Water Institute (Pune, India), Bharathi Integrated Rural Development Society, Edition- illustrated, Publisher-Academic Foundation, 2006.

Tahseen, Rana. *Education and Modernisation of Muslims in India*. New Delhi: Deep and Deep, 1993.

Talwar, S.N. *Under the Banyan Tree: The Communist Movement in India, 1920-1964*. New Delhi: Allied, 1985.

United Nations. Legal Department. *Statement of Treaties and International Agreements Registered or Filed and Recorded with the Secretariat, 548*. New York: 1965.

Vincent, Rose, ed. *The French in India: From Diamond Traders to Sanskrit Scholars*. Trans., Latika Padgaonkar. Bombay: Popular Prakashan, 1990.

Washbrook, David A. *The Emergence of Provincial Politics: The Madras Presidency, 1870-1920*. Cambridge: Cambridge University Press, 1976.

Index